EVERY STUDENT'S GUIDE TO THE WORLD WIDE WEB

FEATURING NETSCAPE NAVIGATOR 2.0

The McGraw-Hill Companies, Inc.

New York   St. Louis
San Francisco   Auckland
Bogotá   Caracas   Lisbon
London   Madrid
Mexico City
Montreal   Milan
New Delhi   San Juan
Singapore   Sydney
Tokyo   Toronto

KEIKO PITTER
ROBERT MINATO

McGraw-Hill

A Division of The **McGraw·Hill** *Companies*

Every Student's Guide to the World Wide Web

1 2 3 4 5 6 7 8 9 0   FGR FGR   9 0 9 8 7 6

ISBN 0–07–052232-4

Sponsoring editor: Frank Ruggirello
Editorial assistant: Kyle Thomes
Technical reviewer: LoriLee Sadler
Production supervisor: Natalie Durbin
Project manager: Cecelia G. Morales
Copyeditor: Maggie Jarpey
Cover designer: Janet Bollow
Compositor: Arizona Publication Service
Printer and binder: Quebecor Printing Fairfield, Inc.

Library of Congress Card Catalog No. 95-81012

CONTENTS

Preface   ix

CHAPTER 1   INTRODUCTION TO THE INTERNET
             AND THE WORLD WIDE WEB   1

✦ Objectives   1
Cyberspace and the 'Net   1
The Internet   2
Finding Information on the 'Net   3
The Client/Server Model   4
Why Mosaic?   5
Then Came Netscape   5
The Web Lingo   7
The Limitations of the Web and Netscape   7
Netiquette   8
Warning   8
Summary   11
Key Terms   11
Review Questions   11
Discussion Topics   12
✦ Box 1.1: Chatting on the 'Net   6
✦ Box 1.2: The Core Rules of Netiquette   9

CHAPTER 2   ACCESSING A WEB SITE   13

✦ Objectives   13
Using the Web   13

The Anatomy of a Web Page   15
A Web URL   20
Going Directly to an URL   20
Subject-Oriented Catalogs of Information   21
Bookmarks   23
Keyword-Oriented Indexes   24
Summary   27
Key Terms   28
Review Questions   28
Exercises   28
Discussion Topics   29
✦ Box 2.1: Domain Name and IP Address   18
✦ Box 2.2: Boolean Search   26

CHAPTER 3   **GOPHER**   **31**

✦ Objectives   31
What's a Gopher?   31
Gopher URL   32
The Gopher Menu   34
Browsing GopherSpace   35
Subject Trees   36
Using Search Tools   38
Summary   43
Key Terms   44
Review Questions   44
Exercises   44
Discussion Topics   45
✦ Box 3.1: Well-Constructed Subject Trees   35
✦ Box 3.2: Other Notable Gopher Sites   42

CHAPTER 4   **FTP**   **47**

✦ Objectives   47
Why Would I Want to Use FTP?   47
FTP URL   48
The FTP Menu   49
Moving Around   50
Archie: User-Index of Anonymous FTP   53

Using Archie   53
Retrieving a File   57
Summary   57
Key Terms   58
Review Questions   58
Exercises   58
Discussion Topics   59
◆ Box 4.1: Using FTP to Obtain Software   48

CHAPTER 5   **TELNET   6 1**

◆ Objectives   61
What Is Telnet?   61
Why Would I Use Telnet?   62
Telnet URL   63
A Telnet Session   63
User Names and Terminal Emulation   67
Hytelnet: Where's the Phone Book?   68
Summary   74
Key Terms   75
Review Questions   75
Exercises   75
Discussion Topics   76
◆ Box 5.1: Is Anybody Home?   64

CHAPTER 6   **E-MAIL   7 7**

◆ Objectives   77
What Is E-Mail?   77
Sending E-Mail Messages   79
E-Mail URL   79
Anatomy of an E-Mail Message   80
Composing and Sending a Message   81
Finding E-Mail Addresses   82
Effective Use of E-Mail   83
Using the E-Mail Feature of Netscape   85
Summary   90
Key Terms   90

Review Questions   90
Exercises   91
Discussion Topics   91
◆ Box 6.1: POP Mail Servers   78
◆ Box 6.2: How to Send E-Mail to Another Network Mail System   82
◆ Box 6.3: Making Faces   84

CHAPTER 7   USENET NEWSGROUPS   93

◆ Objectives   93
What's Usenet?   93
Who Manages Newsgroups?   94
Newsgroup Organization   95
Using the Newsgroups Feature   96
Starting the Newsgroups Feature   96
Finding Newsgroups of Interest   97
Opening a Newsgroup   99
Reading an Article   101
Responding to an Article   102
Posting a New Article   103
Quitting Newsgroups   103
Words of Advice   103
Summary   105
Key Terms   105
Review Questions   105
Exercises   106
Discussion Topics   106
◆ Box 7.1: Just the FAQs, Jack   104

CHAPTER 8   CREATING YOUR OWN WEB PAGE   107

◆ Objectives   107
Hypertext Mark-up Language   107
Creating a Web Document   110
Creating Links   115
Adding Images   117
Design Issues for the Home Page   120
Copyright and Other Laws in Cyberspace   122
Summary   122
Key Terms   123

Review Questions   123
Exercises   123
Discussion Topics   124
✦ Box 8.1: GIF Files   118

Appendix   125

Glossary   137

Index   143

PREFACE

The Internet, or the 'net, is one of the most powerful communication and information resources in existence today. It gives millions of people around the world access to current and archived information on a multitude of topics, and is already proving to be a tremendous help to people—but to students in particular. The World Wide Web, or the Web, is a way of accessing information on the 'net. Netscape is one of the many "browsers" available—programs that you use to utilize the Web.

Every Student's Guide to the World Wide Web is a book about the Web, not a book about the 'net. Although it is true that the Web is probably one of the best ways available today to explore, search, and locate information on the 'net, it does not cover every aspect of the 'net—meaning you cannot find all information on the 'net using the Web. If you are interested in learning things you can do on the 'net, you may want to look at a companion book, *Every Students Guide to the Internet*.

The Web, particularly when using Netscape, tries to accommodate every popular use of the 'net, including Gopher, FTP, Telnet, newsgroups, and even e-mail. The Web does a good job performing some of these tasks, but not all of them. For example, you can Telnet or send e-mail but only if you have a good Telnet or e-mail program installed on your computer. Both the features and limitations of the Web and Netscape Navigator 2.0 are addressed in this text.

The goal of this book is to explain the underlying concepts and strategies involved in locating resources in the constantly shifting landscape of the 'net. Written specifically for college and high school students, no matter what their field of study, the book can be used for short courses or training workshops on the use of the Web to access information on the Internet. It can also be used as a supplement to courses in introductory computing, freshman orientation, and so on.

The material is organized so it can be used for teaching in the classroom or as a self-paced course. Each chapter begins with a list of objectives, and ends with a chapter summary, a list of key terms, review questions, online exercises, and discussion topics. Finally, helpful hints on installing and configuring the Netscape program are followed by a glossary.

Whenever possible, educational examples are used so students can relate concepts easily to their immediate environment. We hope to instill in readers a sense of excitement about the 'net, as well as giving them the ability to use it effectively.

Benefits of using this book are as follows:

✦ The text is simply written, with the beginner in mind, to teach students not only how to access various types of information but also the strategies for finding and using resources.

✦ Online resources at Willamette University were created specifically for use with the book: an e-mail address to which students can send messages for practice and a Web page (http://www.willamette.edu/~kpitter/esgtw.html) to supplement online exercises.

✦ Online Internet support is provided in which students can receive help by sending e-mail messages to the authors:

Keiko Pitter   kpitter@willamette.edu
Robert Minato   rminato@willamette.edu

✦ An appendix offers assistance with Netscape installation and configuration.

✦ The glossary at the end of the book explains 'net and Web terminology.

OUR STRATEGY

The greatest challenge in writing a book like this is presented by the dynamic nature of the Internet. Available resources and the popularity of tools on the Internet change daily. We therefore believe it is important to teach the basic concepts behind each tool so students can adapt to any platform and any tool that will be available in the future. At the same time, we set up a relatively stable environment through the computing center at Willamette University, where Keiko Pitter is the senior director, for students to access both for practice now and for use in the future.

We assume readers have minimal technical experience. However, we also assume they are familiar with the use of a PC and Windows or a Macintosh, and know how to operate a mouse or use the keyboard to make a selection on the screen. The reader must also have an account on an Internet host computer and must have the Web browser, Netscape Navigator 2.0, installed on the computer he or she is using. Look in the Appendix for the system and connection requirements.

ACKNOWLEDGMENTS

We wish to thank Barbara Johnson of the University of Connecticut and LoriLee Sadler of Indiana University for their input. We also want to thank administrators, students, and staff of the Willamette University for their ongoing support and Frank Ruggirello of McGraw-Hill for his trust in us.

INTRODUCTION TO THE INTERNET AND THE WORLD WIDE WEB

1

CHAPTER

OBJECTIVES

Upon completing the material presented in this chapter, you should understand the following aspects of the Internet and the World Wide Web:

✦ The concept behind cyberspace

✦ The concept behind the Internet

✦ The concept behind the World Wide Web

✦ The operation of a client/server model and a Web browser

✦ The terminology used when working with the Web

✦ Guidelines for behavior on the 'net

CYBERSPACE AND THE 'NET

According to William Gibson, who invented the term in his cyberpunk novel *Neuromancer, cyberspace* is "the mass consensual hallucination in which humans all over the planet meet, converse, and exchange information." Like many phenomena predicted in science fiction that have come true, cyberspace is in existence today. People from all over the world, through the use of computers and networks, are communicating and exchanging information in this place that exists only in our minds. Some people refer to cyberspace as the *'net,* and others as the *matrix.* The word **'net** came from *Internet*—the network of networks that connects over 3.2 million computers and some 25 to 30 million users worldwide, and the **matrix** refers to all communication networks, including the Internet and online services such as CompuServe.

THE INTERNET

The idea of creating a network of computers started in the 1960s as a way to distribute and exchange data between military institutes and research and educational institutions in the country. One of the problems in connecting computers was to make sure that the computers talk the same language. The solution was to have a network standard for communication. Any text or data put on the network would be translated into a standard format, or **protocol**, before being transmitted. Information received by a computer would be translated back into its native format. This allowed anyone with a computer supporting the network protocol to connect to the network. The first network was the ARPANET developed by the Department of Defense to make sure that there were several ways to send information from one computer to another, so that if one path broke down, users would have alternative paths available. The ARPANET was more like a *web* or mesh than computers daisy-chained together.

What we know as the Internet arose in the 1980s with the creation of a protocol called **Transfer Control Protocol/Internet Protocol (TCP/IP)** to connect computer networks, and with the National Science Foundation's creation of the NSFNET to link supercomputing centers together. Any computer or network that connects to the Internet must support TCP/IP. That means the computers must speak TCP/IP or be connected to devices that translate their language into TCP/IP. In order for your Macintosh to directly communicate on the Internet, for example, it must be able to speak TCP/IP and hence needs a program called MacTCP. A Windows-based machine needs a similar program, called Winsock.

The Internet does not have a central administrative body. It grows as more computers and networks connect to it. Once you are connected to it, there is much you can do: You can send and receive electronic mail, or *e-mail,* to other users on the Internet and on most online services; you can join electronic discussion groups on Usenet on just about any topic you are interested in; you can use Telnet to log onto a remote computer; you can use FTP to transfer files and documents to and from other computers on the 'net; and you can locate all sorts of information found somewhere on the 'net.

FINDING INFORMATION ON THE 'NET

The Internet is quite different from an online service that is dedicated to the people connected to it. The online service has one large computer system with lots of telephone connections, and the computer provides services to everyone who connects to it. Furthermore, the online service provider makes sure that available services are published and are easy to access.

On the Internet, things are not quite the same. As mentioned earlier, the Internet connects more than 3.2 million computers *worldwide* in a *weblike* structure. Not all of these computers are dedicated to providing service to other people who connect to it remotely—most of these computers have their own things to do, such as compiling software, keeping inventory, and so on. Usually, however, these computers leave a bit of their resources for use or access by other people.

When the Internet was small, finding information or resources on other computers connected to it wasn't too difficult. You looked at your notes or asked someone to find out which computer had the information, and you connected to that computer. However, as the number of computers grew, it was simply impossible to keep a basic catalog of what was on each one. Also, the tools that were available to access other computers or retrieve information from other computers were very primitive. Even if a user knew where the information was, it was often difficult to figure out the program used to retrieve the information.

In late 1989 the CERN High Energy Physics Lab in Switzerland proposed to develop a system to take advantage of computer networking so as to allow researchers to share information with each other. There was already a huge amount of data in the lab, but navigating the data was not always easy. You might, for instance, be reading a report that referred to a set of data located somewhere else than the report. In order to look at the data, you would probably have to jump through several hoops with some other program, finding and then retrieving the desired information. Once you finally had it, it was often not simple to keep track of it for later reference.

The goal of the CERN project was to provide a single interface to many kinds of information, and to be able to link them together. The approach —the World Wide Web proposal—was a concept called **hypertext**, which may be defined as text that links documents together.

Hypertext has its roots in a 1945 article in the *Atlantic* called "As We May Think," by Vannevar Bush, in which he describes a machine he calls *memex* that has turned out to be an accurate prediction for the computer today. Bush predicted that the challenge of the future (today) would be no longer to make new discoveries, but instead to make sense of the huge amount of information already gathered. A memex was like a secretary, storing information and, more importantly, storing connections between pieces of information. By making connections—associations—among related ideas and information, the memex could help you find the specific information you sought. You would simply start with a related concept, and follow the most promising "scent" until you came to what you needed!

The word *hypertext* was not coined until the late 1960s by Ted Nelson. Nelson was fascinated by the machine described by Bush and wrote a pair of books, *Computer Lib* and *Dream Machines*, that laid out in great detail his vision of the future of computers and the future of hypertext. His vision has yet to be realized (he continues to work on Xanadu, which he first proposed in *Dream Machines*), but some claim that the World Wide Web comes awfully close.

So what, then, was the fate of the 1989 proposal at CERN? As you may well have guessed, the proposal was approved, and construction was soon underway on the software to support this scheme. By late 1991 software was available to the Internet community, and the World Wide Web (WWW), or the Web, was born. However, it wasn't until 1993 that the Web began to really take off, with the development of some really slick *client software*, including Mosaic and Netscape.

THE CLIENT/SERVER MODEL

The World Wide Web is based on a **client/server model** that allows for a special relationship between the computer you are using (such as a Macintosh, a PC, or a UNIX workstation) and the (possibly remote) computer that has the information you seek.

✦ The *client program* runs on the computer you are using. It facilitates your access to information by doing the behind-the-scenes work of opening connections to distant computers, sending your request, and receiving and displaying results.

✦ The *server software* runs on the computers that provide the information. A server is often a powerful computer capable of handling information requests from many clients simultaneously.

When a tool is said to follow the client/server model, this implies two things about its function and dependability. The first is that unless you can access a computer that is installed with a client software, you cannot access the server. The second is that a client depends on a server being available to provide information. If the server computer is inoperative, for example, the client cannot access the information. If a server is under a heavy load of many client requests, its response will be very slow.

You can get a version of client software to run on almost any **platform**, which refers to the kind of hardware and operating system used by the computer. UNIX is a platform. A personal computer that utilizes Microsoft Windows is a different platform. The Macintosh computer system is yet another platform. The platform that you use influences what your client software will be like. Macintosh and Windows clients will have the same kind of "friendly" user interface that they are accustomed to from other Macintosh and Windows software products. That is, the user interface will be very visual, commands will be available on a menu bar, and information will appear in windows and dialog boxes on the screen. UNIX clients will have the flavor of UNIX machines: The display is text-based, commands are typed at a prompt, and there is generally only one thing on the screen at a time.

The Web client software, often referred to as a Web **browser**, includes Lynx for the UNIX platform and Mosaic and Netscape for the Macintosh, Windows, and X Windows platforms. In fact, it was Mosaic that led the way to the exploding popularity of the Web today.

WHY MOSAIC?

Mosaic was developed by a group of computer science students at the University of Illinois' National Center for Supercomputing (NCSA) in 1993. It was designed to be an easy-to-use, easy-to-build hypermedia system operated in a graphical interface mode. That is, it utilized pop-up windows, pull-down menus, and "point-and-click" navigation—something all Mac and Windows users were used to. Not only that, but Mosaic was made available to the Internet community free of charge! Another thing Mosaic did was to support audio, movies, graphics, and binary files—something Lynx, its predecessor on the UNIX platform, was not able to do. Mosaic redefined both the World Wide Web and how people used the Internet.

At the same time, Mosaic was not without some problems. For example, it was very difficult to set up and configure Mosaic, it was slow over the conventional modem connection, and it had some bugs.

THEN CAME NETSCAPE

In late 1994 most of the team that wrote NCSA Mosaic, and were now working for Netscape Communications, wrote a second-generation Mosaic. The program was called the *Netscape Navigator,* generally referred to as **Netscape**.

As you might have guessed, Netscape installs easily, is supported by a professional software company, and works well over a conventional modem connection. In addition, it extends the functionality of Mosaic by including most of the services people use on the Internet, such as FTP, Telnet, e-mail, and newsgroups. That means a user need only know how to use Netscape to navigate the 'net effectively!

The program is free to educational institutions and hence it has become the browser of choice in the educational community. However, Netscape also provides a layer of security for the information it reads and sends out, thus offering a safe way to buy and sell things through the Web with a credit card. This feature helped raise interest in the use of the 'net by commercial institutions.

BOX 1.1

CHATTING ON THE 'NET

It's possible to have a conversation, a business meeting, or even a cocktail party on the 'net if you're willing to type instead of actually speaking with other people. Many 'net veterans have used the UNIX Talk program for direct communication with someone else who is logged onto an Internet host computer. The group version of talk, known as *chat,* allows a group of people to talk to each other at once, or to engage in a one-on-one dialog after meeting in a *chat room.*

Chat sessions tend to be open, with participants discussing all sorts of topics, but some have a more specific focus, are restricted to certain topics, or are moderated discussions. The chat room is a popular service offered by many of the commercial online services.

Internet Relay Chat, or IRC, is such a service on the 'net. There are a number of IRC servers around the world through which users can connect and join the discussion of their choice or start a personal conversation with someone else who is also connected to the IRC server. IRC seems a bit like a mix of e-mail and newsgroup, although all conversations take place in "real time" the way telephone conversations and conference calls take place.

At the time this book was being written, Netscape Corporation had just released the beta version of Netscape Chat for Windows. Netscape Chat has the look and feel of the Windows interface and is integrated with Netscape Navigator. With Netscape Chat, users can share information found on the Web as they participate in chat sessions.

You can get more information about the Netscape Chat via Netscape's home page at http://home.netscape.com/. You can also look at the newsgroup *alt.irc* to learn more about other IRC clients.

THE WEB LINGO

When people talk about the Web, they use the following terms, among others: page, home page, links, HTML, and URL. These terms will become clear to you as you work through this book. However, here's a brief description of each.

A **page** is a Web screen. When you use a Web browser and access information, the screen that is displayed—the combination of text, graphics, and links you see on the screen—is the page. **Links** are words or sentences that are underlined to indicate a connection to further resources (a graphic also can be a link). The **home page** is the first screen you see, or the top level of information at a particular site. When you use the Web, you start from the home page of a particular site and you select a link to another page—whether it be at the same location or anywhere in the world. Each screen is like a page in a book. The only difference from a conventional book is that when you find a link that seems interesting, you can go directly to the page that the link points to (whether it is in the same book or in a different book). After you read the new page, you can come back to the original page, or follow yet another link.

The location of each page is defined using something called the **Uniform Resource Locator**, or **URL**. An URL provides complete information about finding a particular resource, no matter what its format, on the Internet. In fact, if you know the URL for a particular resource, you can go directly there without having to follow links from a home page. The format of an URL varies somewhat depending on the resource type. These variations will be explained in each chapter.

HyperText Mark-up Language (HTML) is the language used in the World Wide Web to create documents. In Chapter 8, you will have a chance to create your own Web page using HTML.

THE LIMITATIONS OF THE WEB AND NETSCAPE

Although the Web is one of the best tools to locate all the varying types of resources on the 'net, it does not take the place of all other tools. For example, unless a Telnet program is installed on your computer, it cannot perform the Telnet function, and without a POP mail server, you cannot read incoming e-mail. If you want to perform these functions, you will need to learn how to use your Telnet program and have the system administrator install a POP mail server.

Because the Web lists these various resources as menu options, along with the Web resources, you need to be able to identify the type of located resource (e.g., Web, FTP, Gopher, newsgroup) and make the most effective use of that type of resource.

Although this book uses Netscape, nearly all of the explanations presented here apply to other Web browsers, both on Mac, Windows, and even on UNIX. While the specifics of how a command is given may vary, the strategies involved in finding information will not change.

NETIQUETTE

As you navigate through the 'net, you will notice that it contains many different cultures—called *virtual communities*—where people can find others with interests similar to their own or investigate a body of information they find intriguing. For the most part, these are logical communities, without geographical boundaries or limitations. People in cyberspace come from all walks of life and from all geographical locations. Each brings with him or her a real culture—prejudice, traditions, and all.

Cyberspace is a private space in that you can sit alone in front of your computer to explore areas of interest and yet very public in that once you are in cyberspace, you are surrounded by millions of people and governed by the rules and traditions of each virtual community. Cyberspace is where the computer culture—often based on the technological limits of cyberspace—and common courtesy taken from the noncomputer world are mixed to form a special kind of etiquette: network etiquette, or *netiquette.* If you don't bother learning the conventions of cyberspace, you can embarrass yourself or end up offending someone in ways you never intended.

When you start off in cyberspace, or for that matter, any time you enter a new area of cyberspace, it is a good idea to **lurk**, or look around for a bit to learn the culture.

WARNING

One characteristic of the Internet that warrants a warning is its dynamic nature. Computers make it astoundingly easy to move data, change interfaces, and set up and take down services, and you will find that these things happen frequently. In a library, you can be reasonably assured that the same books, periodicals, and reference works will be there for weeks and months, but the status of services and tools on the Internet is in constant flux.

When using this book and the Internet, you should be mindful of this potential for rapid change. You may find the screen actually displayed to be radically different from what is shown in this book, or you may find a resource referenced here to be nonexistent.

BOX 1.2

THE CORE RULES OF NETIQUETTE

Rule 1. Remember the human.
Never forget that the person reading your mail or posting is, indeed, a person, with feelings that can be hurt.

Corollary 1: It's not nice to hurt other people's feelings.
Corollary 2: Never mail or post anything you wouldn't say to your reader's face.
Corollary 3: Notify your readers when flaming.

Rule 2. Adhere to the same standards of behavior online that you follow in real life.
Corollary 1: Be ethical.
Corollary 2: Breaking the law is bad netiquette.

Rule 3. Know where you are in cyberspace.
Corollary 1: Netiquette varies from domain to domain.
Corollary 2: Lurk before you leap.

Rule 4. Respect other people's time and bandwidth.
Corollary 1: It's okay to think that what you're doing at the moment is the most important thing in the universe, but don't expect anyone else to agree with you.
Corollary 2: Post messages to the appropriate discussion group.
Corollary 3: Try not to ask stupid questions on discussion groups.
Corollary 4: Read the FAQ (Frequently Asked Questions) document.
Corollary 5: When appropriate, use private e-mail instead of posting to the group.
Corollary 6: Don't post subscribe, unsubscribe, or FAQ requests.
Corollary 7: Don't waste expert readers' time by posting basic information.
Corollary 8: If you disagree with the premise of a particular discussion group, don't waste the time and bandwidth of the members by telling them how stupid they are. Just stay away.
Corollary 9: Conserve bandwidth when you retrieve information from a host or server.

Rule 5. Make yourself look good online.
Corollary 1: Check grammar and spelling before you post.
Corollary 2: Know what you're talking about and make sense.
Corollary 3: Don't post flame-bait.

Continued on next page

BOX 1.2	**THE CORE RULES OF NETIQUETTE** (*continued*)

Rule 6. Share expert knowledge.

Corollary 1: Offer answers and help to people who ask questions on discussion groups.

Corollary 2: If you've received e-mail answers to a posted question, summarize them and post the summary to the discussion group.

Rule 7. Help keep flame wars under control.

Corollary 1: Don't respond to flame-bait.

Corollary 2: Don't post spelling or grammar flames.

Corollary 3: If you've posted flame-bait or perpetuated a flame war, apologize.

Rule 8. Respect other people's privacy.

Don't read other people's private e-mail.

Rule 9. Don't abuse your power.

The more power you have, the more important it is that you use it well.

Rule 10. Be forgiving of other people's mistakes.

You were a network newbie once too!

Excerpted with permission from *Netiquette* by Virginia Shea (ISBN 0-9637025-1-3, Albion Books, +1 800-752-7680, info@albion.com).

You need to adapt to change and be able to take alternative actions. If one site is not available for use, then find and use another, similar computer site. If a link or menu option no longer exists, look around to see what you can use instead. You must be patient and willing to make the fluidity of the Internet work for you, instead of being paralyzed by constant change. As you study this book, rather than concentrating on specific sites, you should strive to understand the concept behind each type of information and learn the strategy that will lead you to the information you seek.

Another aspect of the 'net that warrants a warning is the authenticity of its information. There has always been a general misconception about computers and information generated by computers: "If the computer said so, it must be true." This is doubly a misconception for the 'net.

Remember, when you read discussion groups, much of what is being said is "opinion," not fact. Sometimes when you retrieve a document, you find that it is a draft of a student's term paper. Programs such as Netscape make it very easy for anyone to publish information on the 'net. As a librarian once said, "You need to always look at the source of information to determine the authenticity." If a Web page is published by the White House, for example, you can assume the information is valid. But, in general, before you start quoting information found on the 'net, double-check its authenticity.

SUMMARY

In this chapter, many of the terms and concepts that are necessary to use the Internet and the Web were introduced:

✦ Cyberspace is a virtual world created by the use of computers—where people interact with each other via computers and networks.

✦ The Internet is composed of networks and computers supporting a common data transmission protocol called TCP/IP.

✦ The World Wide Web uses a concept called hypertext to link related information.

✦ Mosaic and Netscape are two of the browsers developed to be used with the World Wide Web.

✦ It is important to be respectful of other users on the Internet and follow the netiquette.

✦ The Internet is in constant flux, and it pays to keep abreast of changes so that you can continue to use it even if your sources change.

KEY TERMS

browser	links	page
client/server model	lurk	platform
home page	matrix	protocol
HyperText Mark-up	Mosaic	Transfer Control Protocol/
Language (HTML)	'net	Internet Protocol (TCP/IP)
hypertext	Netscape	Uniform Resource Locator (URL)

REVIEW QUESTIONS

1. What is the Internet?

2. What type of resources can you find on the Internet?

3. What does the Department of Defense have to do with the Internet?

4. What is hypertext?

5. What is a client/server model?

6. What is a platform? What does it mean when someone refers to a "client for a particular platform"?

7. Define the following Web terminology: page, link, and URL.

8. What is the difference between Mosaic and Netscape?

9. What is HyperText Mark-up Language?

10. How stable are the resources and services on the Internet? Explain.

DISCUSSION TOPICS

1. From the brief overview presented in the chapter, how could using the Internet change your daily life and your academic pursuits? What impact could this have on students and faculty in general?

2. If there weren't an Internet or any kind of computer network connecting educational institutions, how might your academic experience change? What would be the impact on academics in general?

3. Why is it a good idea to lurk in cyberspace?

4. What kinds of information would you like to find on the Internet? Keep these things in mind as you move through the book. You may just run across them!

ACCESSING A WEB SITE

2

CHAPTER

Upon completing the material presented in this chapter, you should understand the following aspects of the Web:

✦ How to start Netscape
✦ How to follow a link
✦ How to open a Uniform Resource Locator (URL)
✦ How to find information on a specific topic
✦ How to perform subject-oriented searches using the Web
✦ How to perform index searches using the Web

USING THE WEB

In the last chapter, you patiently read through the discussion of the Internet and the Web. It is time for you to get your hands on them.

In order to use the Web, you need to know how to do the following: start a Web client software; recognize and select links; follow the link; go back to the previous page; specify a Uniform Resource Locator (URL) to open; and exit the Web.

The Web client software you will be using here is Netscape Navigator 2.0, developed by Netscape Communications Corporation (this text was written using a beta version). Netscape is a commercial program, but it is free for academic users (including students). Versions of Netscape for Windows and Macintosh platforms are virtually identical.

NOTE: Even if you are using a browser other than Netscape Navigator 2.0, you will find that most of the explanation here applies to your browser. While the specifics of how a command is given may vary, the strategies involved in finding information will not change.

 Windows Users: In the Program Manager window, visually locate the Netscape icon.

Mac Users: In the Macintosh finder, visually locate the Netscape icon.

Netscape

To start Netscape, double-click on the Netscape icon. Windows users may need to maximize the Netscape window.

The home page, or opening screen, for a Web server is displayed. The page that is displayed is the one to which your copy of Netscape software has been configured. Your display may look similar to the one shown in Figure 2.1.

Figure 2.1 is the Welcome page for Netscape Communications. Although most documents on the Web will contain similar elements, you may want to display the

FIGURE 2.1

same screen as Figure 2.1. You can do this by opening the File menu and selecting Open Location. Type **http://home.netscape.com/** in the dialog box.

THE ANATOMY OF A WEB PAGE

No matter what browser you are using, there are some common visual elements in a Web page. You will find that these are very similar to a page in a book.

Headings	On a Web page, there is usually a *heading* at the top. Also, there are *subheadings* that break up the contents of the page into readable groups.
Text	A Web page is not just a list of topics. It usually contains *text* to explain contents or links.
Graphics	A Web page contains a lot of *graphics*—pictures, icons, cartoons, or whatever. Because graphics can take some time to load, some browsers can be set so that graphics do not load automatically.
Links	*Links* are what make a Web so special. Underlined words are links embedded in the text that lead to other information resources. However, links can also be graphic images. When you place the mouse pointer on top of these links, the mouse pointer turns into a pointing finger and the link destination is displayed in the status message. To follow the link, you just click on it.

Figure 2.2 labels various parts of a Netscape Web page. For example, immediately below the menu is a series of buttons called the Toolbar that allows you to do things like move back to a previous document and find text in the document you are currently in, or return to the home page from which you started. Below this, your current location (labeled "Location" or "Netsite") is displayed in the form of an URL.

NOTE: The box is labeled "Netsite" when the server being accessed is a Netscape Web server, and "Location" when it was created using other Web management software.

Finally, the Directory buttons such as What's New, Net Search, and Net Directory are displayed.

NOTE: If you do not see a Toolbar, Location (Netsite), and/or Directory button, select the Options menu. A pull-down menu, as shown in Figure 2.3, appears. To select an option for display, click on it so that a checkmark appears in front of it.

FIGURE 2.2

Tool bar

Location field

Directory buttons

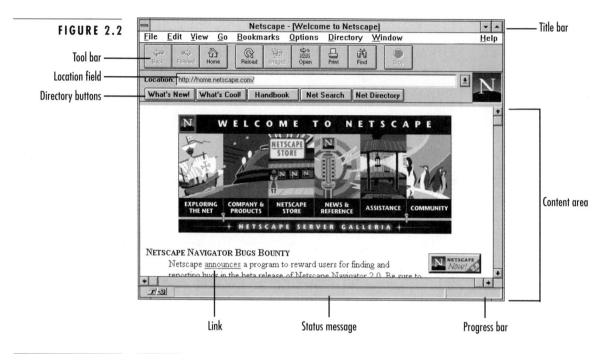

Title bar

Content area

Link   Status message   Progress bar

FIGURE 2.3

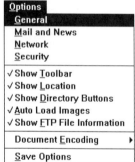

If you want to quit at any time, you do what you do with any Macintosh or Windows application: From the File menu, select Quit or Exit, respectively.

 Scroll down the page until you see a series of menu options (underlined words) as displayed in Figure 2.4.

You can follow any text that appears as an underlined link. As you place your mouse pointer on top of a link, the mouse pointer turns into a pointing finger and you will see where this link points to—the URL of the destination—displayed in the Status message at the bottom.

 Click on a link.

You are taken to a new page. The new location now appears in the Location (Netsite) text box.

FIGURE 2.4

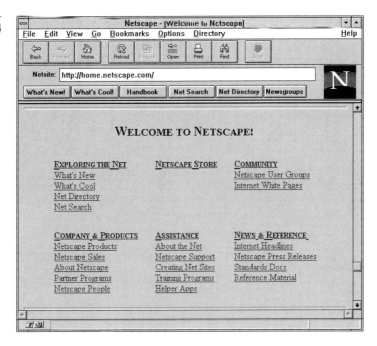

Now, if you select a link in the new page, you will progress even further in the link. You can also go back to the previously visited pages by clicking on the Back button found in the Toolbar.

 Open the Go menu.

The menu shows the titles (not the URL) of all the Web pages you have visited, as shown in Figure 2.5.

The checkmark in front of a listing indicates this as the page currently on display. When you click on the Back button, you proceed to the page listed beneath the current one. The Forward button takes you to the page listed just above the current one. The Home button takes you back to the original home page. Furthermore, you can go to any page listed by dragging the mouse to select it.

FIGURE 2.5

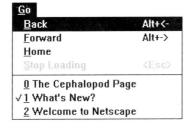

BOX 2.1   DOMAIN NAME AND IP ADDRESS

When a network site wishes to connect to the 'net, a unique range of addresses is assigned to it. The site will use one address for each device on the network. The range of addresses could be large or small depending on the number of devices the site has or anticipates having. Whenever someone wants to access a computer on the site, the person must specify the address of the computer. If someone wants to send e-mail to a user at a site, the sender must specify the user name of the recipient, along with the address of the computer on which the recipient has an account.

To the devices on the network, each address is a number called an **Internet Protocol (IP) address**, usually displayed as a series of four numbers separated by periods. For example, 158.104.1.1 is the IP address of a computer at Willamette University. However, since many people have a hard time remembering numbers, especially large ones, there is usually a name associated with each address. In the early days of the Internet, names and addresses were listed in a file that was passed around the network, but as the number of machines increased, so did the size of the file. And every time a new machine was added to the network, the file became out of date. Consequently, in the modern Internet, a site usually requests, along with its range of addresses, a **domain name**, which is a series of words separated by periods. The site is responsible for any names "under" that domain and for entering in the corresponding address for each name. Willamette University has the domain name willamette.edu, so all machines "under" that domain are managed and named by Willamette University. For example, jupiter.willamette.edu is the name for the address 158.104.1.1 mentioned earlier. (*Note:* In IP addresses and domain names, a period (.) is referred to as a "dot.")

When you use the domain name in accessing a computer on the Internet, the domain name is translated by the Domain Name System into the host's corresponding IP address. In the domain name michael.ai.mit.edu, for example, the Internet host michael is in the domain called ai, which is in the domain mit. That is an educational institution (indicated by edu). In other words, a domain name contains information about the computer system.

Just as mail addresses are subdivided into countries containing smaller units, such as states and cities, domain names are divided into various levels of domains. The last word in the domain name is the *top-level domain,* which can be either the geographic location or the countries and territories in which the host computer is located. They include the following:

Continued on next page

BOX 2.1

DOMAIN NAME AND IP ADDRESS (*continued*)

AQ	Antarctica	IN	India
AR	Argentina	IT	Italy
AT	Austria	JP	Japan
AU	Australia	KR	Korea
BE	Belgium	MX	Mexico
BR	Brazil	NL	The Netherlands
CA	Canada	NO	Norway
CH	Switzerland	NZ	New Zealand
CL	Chile	PR	Puerto Rico
DE	Germany	PT	Portugal
DK	Denmark	SE	Sweden
ES	Spain	SG	Singapore
FI	Finland	TN	Tunisia
FR	France	TW	Taiwan
GR	Greece	UK	United Kingdom
HK	Hong Kong	US	United States
HU	Hungary	VE	Venezuela
IE	Ireland	ZA	South Africa
IL	Israel		

If a geographic location is not specified, it is assumed to be the United States. In fact, within the United States, most network sites use the "organizational" identification for the top-level domain instead.

COM	Commercial organizations
EDU	Educational and research institutions
GOV	Government agencies
MIL	Military agencies
NET	Major network support centers
ORG	Other organizations
INT	International organizations

The second-to-last word gives a descriptive (or nondescriptive!) reference to the organization: you might expect stjude.edu to refer to an educational institution by the name of St. Jude's, nwnet.net to be a network service provider called NWNet, and apple.com to be company called Apple. All other words in the domain name are subdomain within the domain—that is, subdivisions within the organization. For example, jupiter.willamette.edu and mercury.willamette.edu are both computers within the Willamette University network.

A WEB URL

URL stands for Uniform Resource Locator. It is the method used to identify the exact location and format of a resource on the Web. The structure of an URL is divided into three parts: the type, the server, and the path to the specific file.

Type://Server/Directory/File

The *type* for a Web page is http. The *server* is the name of the machine you are accessing. The name is a series of words separated by periods (dots). Many names start with the word "www" followed by the domain name for the machine.

For example, http://www.willamette.edu/ will access the Web server (and main Web page) at Willamette University (domain name willamette.edu). If you are connecting to a particular Web page that is located somewhere on the computer, you need to specify the *directory* (folder) where it is located. Again, http://www.willamette.edu/~kpitter/ will access the home page that is contained in the directory (folder) kpitter. Furthermore, to specify a Web document, say esgti.html, that is contained in the directory (folder) kpitter, the URL is http://www.willamette.edu/~kpitter/esgti.html.

If you ever want to guess the URL for someone's Web page, bear in mind that a typical Web URL starts with "www," and domain names for educational institutions end with .edu, for government agencies with .gov, and for commercial comanies with .com. So if you are trying to reach a Web site for a commercial company—for example Netscape or Apple—you could try **http://www.netscape.com/** or **http://www.apple.com/**. For a government agency like the FBI or the White House, you could try **http://www.fbi.gov/** or **http://www.whitehouse.gov/**. For an educational institution like Yale University or UCLA, you could try **http://www.yale.edu/** or **http://www.ucla.edu/**. Chances are these would work.

NOTE: The format for an URL changes slightly depending on the type of resource. The URL format for e-mail or a newsgroup is quite different from one for, say, a Gopher resource. These various formats are explained in each chapter.

GOING DIRECTLY TO AN URL

When you know the URL of a site you want to view, you can go there directly by entering the URL in the Location (Netsite) text box.

 Type an URL in the Location (Netsite) text box. You can try
http://www.whitehouse.gov/.

The home page for the Web site you selected appears. Figure 2.6 shows the Web page for the White House.

FIGURE 2.6

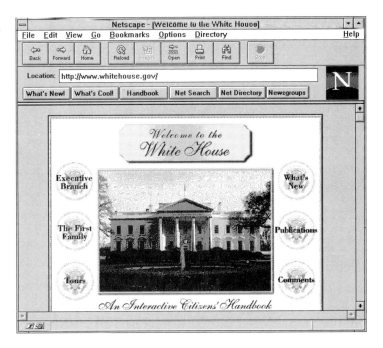

SUBJECT-ORIENTED CATALOGS OF INFORMATION

If you have some subject area you want to explore, Netscape already has a tool for you.

 Click on the Net Directory button.

Netscape's Internet Directory, similar to the one shown in Figure 2.7, appears.

The page displays the subject list from the Yahoo Directory, one of the Internet's resources. One of Yahoo's outstanding features is that users may add new topics and resources to the lists, which means that (in a sense) Yahoo is maintained by the Internet community. At the time this book was written, Yahoo listed more than 44,000 resources.

Let's try the following: You just saw the movie *Apollo 13* and found the story fascinating. In fact, you think that this would be a good topic for your science term paper. Now you need more information on it. The first thing you will try is something logical.

 Select the category of Science in the Yahoo Directory.

Select Aviation and Aeronautics and then select Space.

A screen similar to the one shown in Figure 2.8 is displayed.

FIGURE 2.7

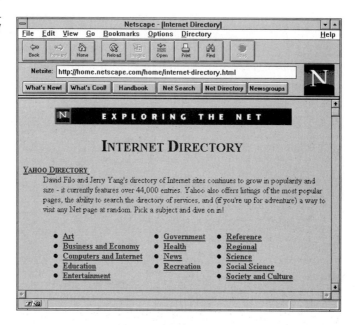

FIGURE 2.8

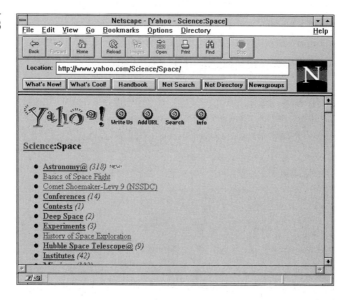

You see a number of topics that may lead to information you seek. You can try Missions or History of Space Exploration.

 **Select History of Space Exploration.**

BINGO, you found it.

NOTE: You might find it interesting that there were other ways to get to the same spot. If you think of this event as "history," then you would start with Humanities as the first choice in the directory. You would then select the following links to get to this same spot: History, ASAP Web - History of Science, Technology, and Medicine, Astronomy and Space, then NASA Kennedy Space Center History Archives.

 Scroll the screen until you see the section for Manned Missions and select Apollo Program.

You see a screen similar to the one shown in Figure 2.9.

You will find all sorts of interesting information about the Apollo Space program, including some images.

It's great that you found some interesting things, but what can you do with them, other than to view the screen? If you want to print what is displayed, just select the File menu, and choose Print. If you want to retrieve the displayed image or text, select the File menu, then choose Save As. Specify the location on your computer where you want to store the file, and the file is transferred. It's that simple. You can try these on your own.

BOOKMARKS

Now that you've found this great resource, it would be handy to be able to find it again without going through all this work. Netscape offers something called **bookmarks** to let you keep track of sites you've visited so that you can reconnect to them quickly. Let's add a bookmark for the Web page of Project Apollo.

FIGURE 2.9

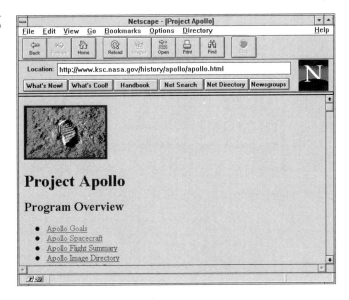

FIGURE 2.10

Bookmarks	
Add Bookmark	Ctrl+A
View Bookmarks...	Ctrl+B
Project Apollo	

Use the Go menu and select Project Apollo.

Project Apollo is displayed.

From the Bookmarks menu, select Add Bookmark.

The item has been added to the bookmark.

Let's check and see.

Open the Bookmarks menu.

The item you just added appears on the Bookmarks menu, as shown in Figure 2.10.

You can connect to the site by dragging the mouse to select it. Bookmarks are a useful tool for keeping track of interesting resources you find when exploring the Internet. But enough about bookmarks, let's get on to the task at hand.

KEYWORD-ORIENTED INDEXES

Another way to find information on a specific subject is through an index. In a book, an index helps you find specific information quickly, without messing around with the table of contents to try to figure out which chapter the information might be in. Similarly, indexes on the Web allow you to use specific **keywords**—words relevant to the information being sought. There are numerous search tools on the Web. You will start with Net Search.

Click on the Net Search button.

Netscape's list of Internet Search tools appears, similar to the one shown in Figure 2.11.

Go to the first search tool, InfoSeek.

Type **Apollo 13** as shown in Figure 2.12, then click on the Run Query button.

The search resulted in several resources being displayed.

Locate the text similar to the following:

Apollo-13
(29).Pad 39-A (7). Saturn-V AS-508 (). High Bay 1. MLP 3. Firing Room 1.
Crew: James A. Lovell, Jr.. John L. Swigert, Jr.. Fred W. Haise, Jr.. Backup
Crew:. Milestones:. 06/13/69- S-IVB on dock at KSC. 06/29/69 - S-II...

----http://www.ksc.nasa.gov/history/apollo/apollo-13/apollo-13.html (17K)

NOTE: You can do this by selecting the Edit menu and choosing Find. Type **Apollo 13**, or other text that is unique on this page, in the text box, and click on Find.

FIGURE 2.11

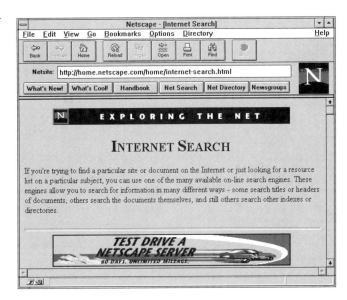

FIGURE 2.12

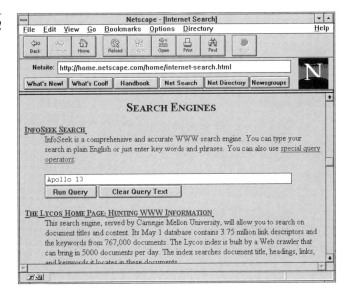

BOX 2.2	**BOOLEAN SEARCH**

Obviously, the choice of a keyword will determine the success of an information search. One other thing that would contribute to success is the appropriate use of Boolean operators. These are the conjunctive words AND, OR, and NOT, which you place between keywords to expand or limit the scope of your search. Many of the search tools on the 'net support the use of Boolean operators.

When you type in more than one word for the search tool to seek, and you don't put an AND, OR, or NOT between the words, most tools assume AND. For example, if you perform a search for "dogs cats" or "dogs AND cats," you will find all resources that have both "dogs" and "cats" in the titles. You've limited the search to entries with both keywords. If you perform a search for "dogs OR cats", the search tool finds those entries that contain either "dogs" or "cats" or both. You will find more things than if you had used "and." Now, if you perform a search for "dogs NOT cats", you will find those entries that contain only "dogs."

You can link together keywords with more than one Boolean operator, and you can use parentheses to separate distinct units: searching for "(dogs AND cats) NOT (frogs OR cars)" would return titles with both "dogs" and "cats," only if those titles did not have either "frogs" or "cars."

You can get really spiffy, and define very exacting searches with Booleans and parentheses. But it usually takes more time to compose a complex search of several keywords than to type in two or three truly relevant keywords.

 Select and follow this link for Apollo 13 (or you can just go to the URL).

A screen similar to the one shown in Figure 2.13 is displayed.

You thought what you found before through the Internet Directory was great. This is even better.

 You may want to add this to the Bookmarks menu as well.

You will find out that as you try different search engines for the same search, different results are displayed. If you don't find what you are looking for after trying one search engine, just try a different one. Eventually you will find the resource you are looking for.

FIGURE 2.13

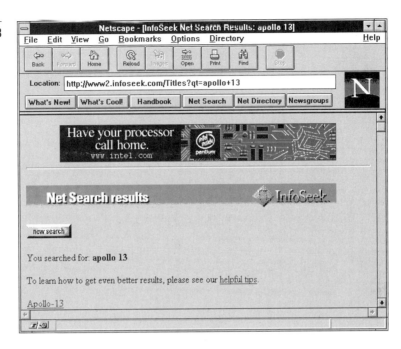

SUMMARY

In this chapter, many of the terms and concepts that are necessary to use the Web were introduced:

✦ Links within a document are identified by an underline. You can select and follow the link by clicking on it once. You can navigate back and forth through links by using the button bar.

✦ You can display a WWW page directly by specifying the Uniform Resource Locator (URL) name in the Location (Netsite) text box.

✦ An URL has the format *Type://Server/Directory/File*, where the *type* for a Web page is http. The *server* is the name of the machine you are accessing.

✦ You can locate a specified text on a Web page by scrolling the page and visually locating it or by using the Find command in the Edit menu.

✦ The Net Directory button and the Yahoo Directory are good places to start a subject-oriented search.

✦ The Net Search button is a good place to start a keyword search.

✦ A feature called Bookmarks can be used to keep track of sites you've visited and would like to reconnect with.

KEY TERMS

bookmarks	Internet Protocol (IP) address	keyword
domain name		

REVIEW QUESTIONS

1. What is the purpose of a link?

2. If an URL has the domain name of www.reed.edu, what type of institution runs the server?

3. How do you connect directly to an URL?

4. In Netscape, how do you recognize, select, and follow a link?

5. In Netscape, how do you find a particular text within the Web page?

6. What would you guess as the URL for a Web home page for a network service provider whose domain name is teleport.com?

7. How do you start a subject-oriented search in Netscape?

8. How do you start a keyword-oriented search in Netscape?

9. Once you locate a document in WWW, what can you do with it?

10. What is the purpose of the Bookmarks feature?

EXERCISES

1. Some of you may soon be facing decisions about which graduate or undergraduate institution to attend. Find a Web resource that can help in making this decision, and describe what you located.

2. Perform a 'net search on the keyword "sound files." Describe resources you located. Name the types of hardware and software that are needed for you to hear sound on the 'net.

3. You often hear about ergonomics issues related to the use of various input and output devices. Perform a 'net search using the keyword "ergonomics," or connect to the Web page for Computer Related Repetition Strain Injuries at http://engr-www.unl.edu/ee/eeshop/rsi.html. Describe some of the issues.

4. Conduct a 'net search to see if you can find the memory requirement for the new Microsoft Windows software. Describe what type of information you found. (Hint: connect to the Web page for Microsoft at http://www.microsoft.com/.)

DISCUSSION TOPICS

1. The sources available in a library can often be trusted as authoritative. One thing that is problematic about online resources is that they are more difficult to validate than library resources. Discuss reasons why this might be.

2. Think of topics about which you may have to write a term paper, and discuss keywords that might be used when conducting a search.

3. What are some Internet skills you need before you can effectively use the Web?

GOPHER

3

CHAPTER

OBJECTIVES

Upon completing the material presented in this chapter, you should understand the following aspects of the Internet and using Gopher on the World Wide Web:

◆ The concept behind Gopher

◆ How to navigate through Gopher menus using Netscape

◆ The meaning of an URL (Uniform Resource Locator) for Gopher sites

◆ The strategies for browsing the World Wide Web via Gopher

◆ How to use Veronica to search for resources

WHAT'S A GOPHER?

Internet experts have recognized for some time that although the 'net is the repository of a vast amount of digital information, it is often too complicated for casual users. In spring of 1991, about the time the idea for the World Wide Web was being proposed and way before the days of Mosaic and Netscape, a team of programmers at the University of Minnesota developed a software tool called Gopher.

Gopher is a consistent, menu-driven interface that allows users to access a large number of varied resources on networks without requiring them to know a lot of arcane computer commands. With Gopher, accessing information on the Internet can be as easy as making a selection on a menu. No matter where you are on the Internet, the interface is always the same. It allows users to locate, see, and retrieve information through the Internet as if it were in folders and menus on their computer. Anyone can make use of the resources available on the Internet by using Gopher.

Although Gopher was initially developed as a tool to allow users at the University of Minnesota to quickly gain access to information available on their campus computer network, within the space of a year Gopher caught on in popularity both as a means of making information available and for accessing information on the Internet. Within two years, there were more than 2,000 registered **Gopher servers**, computer sites where information is made available through the use of Gopher, and doubtless hundreds more that were unregistered or experimental. In fact, the term **GopherSpace** was coined to describe all the menus and information available through Gopher. It is no wonder that the World Wide Web was developed to assure access to GopherSpace. Although it is true that many institutions are now constructing Web pages to disseminate information, there is still a lot of information in GopherSpace.

GOPHER URL

As you make selections on the Web, you can tell if you have selected a Gopher resource by the appearance and by the URL of the resource.

A Gopher page is a list of menu selections. You will notice that every item is a link, either to another menu option or to a document. A Gopher URL has the format *gopher://domain-name:port/path*, where *domain-name* is the name of the Gopher server and *path* is the location within the Gopher server where the information is found. The *port* may or may not be specified. The port refers to a specific communication channel on which the destination computer is waiting for a request. The default port is 70. By entering a port number, you are overriding the default.

You can also directly access a Gopher server by entering the URL in the Location (Netsite) text box, as you can with any URL.

Enter the URL **http://www.willamette.edu/~kpitter/esgtw.html**

A screen similar to the one shown in Figure 3.1 is displayed.

Find the section "Chapter 3."

Position the mouse pointer over Willamette University Gopher.

The URL displayed on the status message at the bottom is gopher://gopher.willamette.edu/, indicating that this link connects you to the Gopher server at Willamette University.

Select the link.

A Gopher screen similar to the one shown in Figure 3.2 is displayed.

FIGURE 3.1

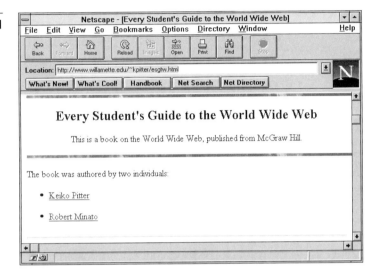

FIGURE 3.2

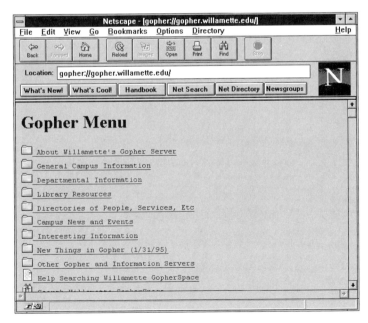

Gopher servers are usually one of two types: a **Campus-Wide Information System (CWIS)** or a general audience information server.

✦ A *CWIS* contains information of interest to the students, faculty, and staff of a particular campus. In addition to the campus-related information, it often contains paths to other Gopher sites.

✦ A *general audience information server* provides information that will be of use to a large group of people with some common interests—for example, the lyrics server at University of Wisconsin.

The Gopher at Willamette University is a CWIS.

THE GOPHER MENU

Information on a Gopher server is organized in a treelike structure: There is a **root Gopher** server (menu) from which you start, with branches leading in all directions. Each menu displays choices that include text files, graphic images, sounds, or other menus, and these resources can reside on computer systems all over the world! Most likely these choices are organized in some kind of subject-related fashion.

On the menu, the type of selection is indicated. In Netscape, icons that precede menu options indicate the selection type. Table 3-1 shows the symbols and their meanings.

TABLE 3-1 NETSCAPE MENU ICONS

ICON	SELECTION TYPE	EXPLANATION
	A file; text to be viewed	A file that can be displayed by nearly every kind of computer. The text is not formatted as it may be on a word processor. The file can be displayed on the screen, then saved, e-mailed to yourself, or printed.
	A directory	When you select this item, another menu is displayed.
	A searchable index or directory search services	A collection of documents that have been fully indexed by every word contained within them, or a search service that helps you locate information about a user or a topic.
	Launches a Telnet session	When you make this selection, you will leave the Gopher program to access a remote computer system. The Gopher client will present a warning as well as information on how to get into and out of the system to which you've Telnetted.
	A binary file	Binary file that cannot be viewed. It can be saved.
	A graphics file	Pictures in various formats, such as GIF. Not all clients can handle this information.
	Digitized sound	Not all clients can handle this information.

BOX 3.1

WELL-CONSTRUCTED SUBJECT TREES

Here is a list of a few Gophers with good subject trees that you may want to try. To connect directly, specify the address. For example, to connect to North Carolina State University, enter **gopher://dewey.lib.ncsu.edu:70/** in the Location (Netsite) box.

Resource	URL

Gopher Jewels at the University of Southern California
    Look in the Other Gophers and Information
    Resources folder for "Gopher Jewels."
	gopher://cwis.usc.edu

Library of Congress Marvel Gopher
    Look in the Global Electronic Library
    folder.
	gopher://marvel.loc.gov

North Carolina State University
    Look in the NCSU's Library Without Walls
    folder for "Study Carrels."
	gopher://dewey.lib.ncsu.edu

RiceInfo Look in the Information by Subject Area folder.	gopher://riceinfo.rice.edu

For a collection of sites that have subject trees, try connecting to:

Michigan State University List of Subject Trees
    Look in the Network & Database Resources
    folder for "Internet Resources by Subject."
	gopher://burrow.cl.msu.edu

BROWSING GOPHERSPACE

When **browsing** through GopherSpace, you make a selection and see what options are displayed next, make another selection and see what happens, and so on, until you find a piece of information that is of interest to you. You discover the menus that someone else has designed to present information. There is often logic and organization to individual menu structures used in Gopher, but for the most part you are exploring the links that connect Gophers and resources. Within the context of GopherSpace, sometimes you have no idea where your menu choices will lead you.

Fortunately, this is where Netscape helps. You can look at the Status message to see the URL of the current Gopher site. You can keep track of where you've been in the Go menu, and you can also use the Bookmark feature to flag Gopher sites you may want to visit again.

With the exercises and examples that follow, you will learn how to select and navigate effectively in GopherSpace. The best way to become familiar with it is to use it. Later in this chapter, you will learn how to use search tools available on Gopher so that you are not just blindly looking for information.

To give you an idea of how Gopher can be used to accomplish a specific research task, you will consider the following scenario:

You are taking a class in Environmental Science and decide to do a paper on Greenpeace. You need all references!

SUBJECT TREES

Although it is true that all Gopher menus are somewhat organized by subject, some sites have invested more time and effort than others in creating menus and organizations that make locating resources on the Internet easier. Such sites are said to have a **subject tree**. You will find these on menu options under a variety of names: subject resources, study carrels, topical resources, Internet Resources by Subject, and so on. All of these indicate an arrangement of resources by some subject scheme. Let's try one. All you need to do is to follow the tree by making selections.

 In the Location (Netsite) text box, type **gopher://burrow.cl.msu.edu** and press ENTER.

You are connected to the Gopher at Michigan State University. The screen should look similar to Figure 3.3.

Select Network & Database Resources, then Internet Resources by Subject.

The subject tree you want to use is still buried. You need to follow whatever subject category you think is logical. If you decide that the selection was not correct, backup and try another path.

 Select Subject Trees, Other Inform. Systems, Internet Resource Clarification.
Select Internet Resources, by Subject.
Select Mathematics, Natural Sciences, and then Environmental Studies.

As you scroll through the screen to look at menu choices, you might notice that there is a Gopher for Greenpeace!

 Select Greenpeace Gopher.

A screen similar to the one shown in Figure 3.4 is displayed.

FIGURE 3.3

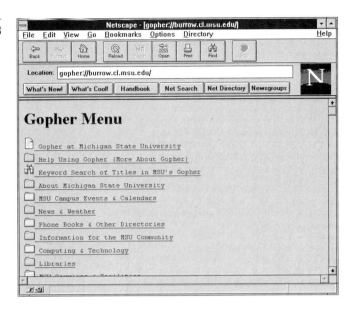

FIGURE 3.4

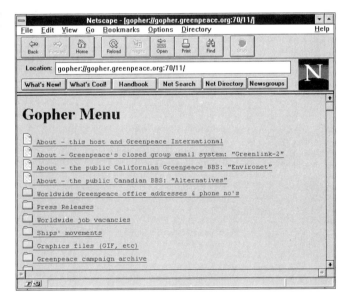

Once you locate a document of interest, you can view it on screen or save the document as a file on your local computer, where you can edit and print it as any other text document. You can save the document by opening the File menu and selecting the Save As command. A dialog box is displayed where you can specify the location where you want the document saved.

USING SEARCH TOOLS

Subject trees are like a table of contents. You can browse specific subject areas to find general information on the topic. But what if you are looking for specific information and don't know exactly where it might be located? In a book, you would use the index; fortunately, Gopher has one, too.

In the fall of 1992 the University of Nevada, Reno, released a program that would search through GopherSpace and index all of the titles it saw. The program is named **Veronica**, an acronym for Very Easy Rodent-Oriented Net-wide Index to Computerized Archives (the pun was hard to resist, since there was another searching tool called Archie).

Veronica has two parts: one that combs the network, maintaining an index of Gopher titles, and another that takes requests on keywords and returns a list of "hits."

First you need to find a Veronica server.

 In the Location (Netsite) text box, type **gopher://gopher.micro.umn.edu** and press ENTER.

The Minnesota Gopher screen similar to the one in Figure 3.5 is displayed.

FIGURE 3.5

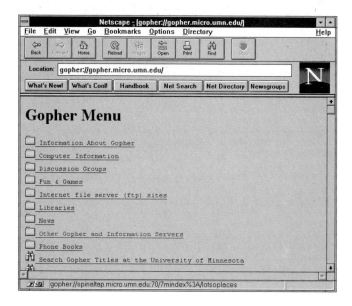

Select Other Gopher and Information Servers.

A menu similar to the one in Figure 3.6 is displayed.

One of the top few options should be Veronica.

 Select Search titles in GopherSpace using veronica.

A menu similar to the one in Figure 3.7 is displayed.

FIGURE 3.6

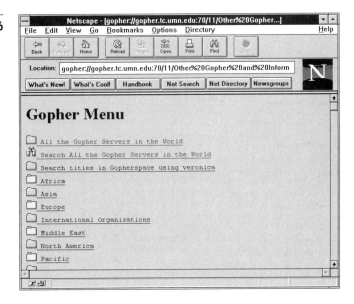

FIGURE 3.7

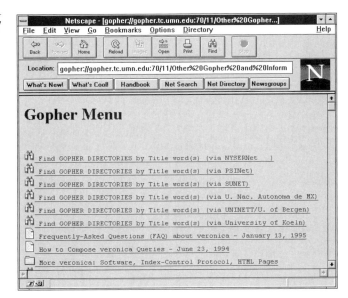

Some of the items are Help files, which include information on new features, *frequently asked questions* (FAQs), and help in composing queries. You will also see three groups of items: Find GOPHER DIRECTORIES by Title words(s), Search GopherSpace by Title word(s), and Simplified Veronica.

The difference between *Simplified Veronica* and the regular Veronica is as follows: although there are several Veronica servers on the Internet, users often receive the message "Too many connections - Try again soon." The user has to then try the search again using another server listed. The Simplified Veronica tries all of the servers and uses one that's not busy!

✦ "Search GopherSpace by Title word(s) . . . and Simplified Veronica: find ALL gopher types" will accept *keywords* you enter to search all the Gopher titles about which the Veronica server knows. This includes any directory, file, search tools, sound file, or Telnet session. If your keyword matches any item at all, the item will be returned to you on a menu.

✦ "Find GOPHER DIRECTORIES by Title word(s) and Simplified Veronica: Find Gopher MENUS only" will accept keywords to search only *titles of folders* in GopherSpace. It ignores all other Gopher items.

So, what's the difference? Let's find out by trying the same keyword in both. If you have problems getting connected to one server, try another. You will go ahead and use Simplified Veronica so you do not have to go searching for a Veronica that's not busy!

Select Simplified Veronica: find ALL gopher types.

A dialog box appears, similar to the one displayed in Figure 3.8, prompting you for keywords.

Click in the keyword text box to position the cursor, type Greenpeace, and press ENTER.

There will be a (usually) brief pause while Veronica is working. You will notice a message at the bottom of the screen indicating the connection attempt. Soon a new menu, similar to the one shown in Figure 3.9, is displayed.

Depending on what you are searching for and the site you chose, the list that is returned may contain a few, or hundreds, of items. You might note by looking at the icons that the information located includes both text files and folders. Out of this mixture, you will find that the majority are irrelevant to your needs. You need to sort through all the selections, but there's just so much.

This is where the "Find GOPHER DIRECTORIES by Title word(s)" or "Simplified Veronica: MENUS only" item is useful. The list returned consists of *directories*

FIGURE 3.8

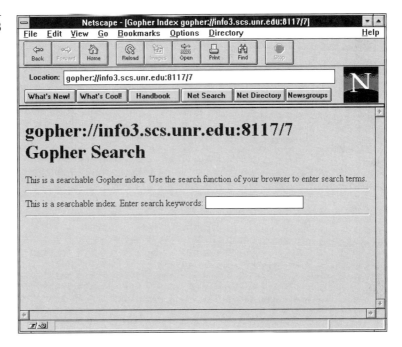

FIGURE 3.9

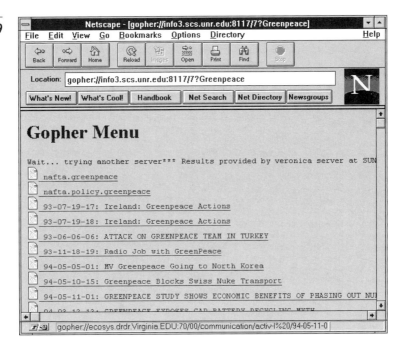

BOX 3.2	OTHER NOTABLE GOPHER SITES

The following is a list of sites you may want to try:

Resource	URL
Coalition for Networked Information	gopher://gopher.cni.org
Electronic Newsstand	gopher://gopher.enews.com
Environmental Protection Agency Gopher	gopher://gopher.epa.gov
The Internet Society	gopher://ietf.CNRI.Reston.Va.US
MARVEL Library of Congress Gopher	gopher://marvel.loc.gov
National Science Foundation Gopher	gopher://stis.nsf.gov
Scholarly Electronic Conferences Look in the Computing folder for "Internet Information."	gopher://gopher.usask.ca:70
United Nations	gopher://nywork1.undp.org
White House Information Including Press Releases—look in the following folders: Browse Information by Subject, Government Information, Information from the White House.	gopher://gopher.tamu.edu
World Health Organization	gopher://gopher.who.ch

(meaning menus that lead to further menus), which should contain a collection of information relevant to the keyword you entered in your search.

 Return to the Search titles in GopherSpace using veronica screen.
Select Simplified Veronica: Find Gopher MENUS only, and enter **Greenpeace** as the keyword.

You should get a menu of returns, all directories, similar to the one shown in Figure 3.10.

Veronica is far from perfect. It searches only titles, and it has no way of determining the content or subject of a particular file in its index. Also, as with any method of searching for information using keywords, the choice of keywords may have dramatic effect on what you find. Suppose we had chosen *environment* or *peace* instead of *Greenpeace*? It's a good idea to try synonyms when using Veronica, especially if you don't seem to be finding information you can use. In addition, Veronica supports Boolean searching. When you enter more than one keyword, Veronica assumes AND. You can use OR or NOT between words to limit or expand the scope of your search (see Box 2.2 in Chapter 2).

 From the File menu, select Exit or Quit.

FIGURE 3.10

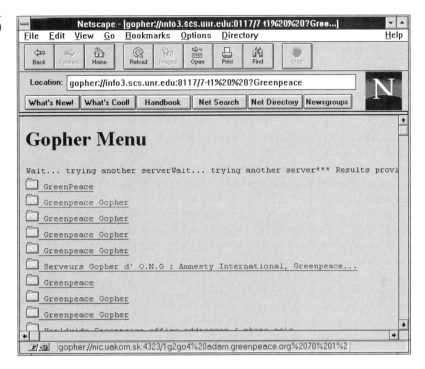

SUMMARY

In this chapter, many of the terms and concepts that are necessary to use Gopher were introduced:

✦ Gopher is a consistent, menu-driven interface accessible through Netscape that allows users to access information on the Internet.

✦ When you browse through GopherSpace, you are making selections as they appear on the menu, depending on the organization as presented in each menu.

✦ A Campus-Wide Information System (CWIS) is used by educational institutions to disseminate information about the campus. Many use Gopher as the tool.

✦ A subject tree is a Gopher menu structure where resources are presented by subject area.

✦ Veronica is a search tool within Gopher. You have a choice of doing a keyword selection to find all documents and resources or just to find directory titles containing the keyword.

KEY TERMS

browsing

Campus-Wide Information
System (CWIS)

Gopher

Gopher server

GopherSpace

root Gopher

subject tree

Veronica

REVIEW QUESTIONS

1. How can you tell if a link on a Web page takes you to a Gopher server?

2. What is the difference between using Gopher from Netscape and a Gopher server program?

3. What is a CWIS?

4. When you run Gopher within Netscape, how do you specify to which Gopher server you'd like to connect?

5. How do you make selections on a Gopher menu?

6. When a Gopher menu selection runs to more than one screen, how do you view the rest of the options?

7. How do you go up a menu structure? That is, after you make a selection from a menu, how do you go back to the previous menu?

8. Why is the subject tree useful?

9. What is Veronica?

10. In Veronica, what is the difference between "Search GopherSpace by Title word(s)" and "Find GOPHER DIRECTORIES by Title word(s)"?

EXERCISES

1. Find and list Gopher resources that pertain to United States Census data.

2. Find out what the National Science Foundation has provided to the Internet community via Gopher. Specify how you found the information. List some resources found.

3. Find Gopher resources that contain collections of electronic journals on women's movements. Describe how you found these journals, and list where they are located.

4. Find a Gopher resource that contains the most up-to-date weather statistics or satellite maps for your area of the world. How far is it from your location to the nearest hurricane or tropical storm? Specify how you found your answer.

DISCUSSION TOPICS

1. Why would you use a Gopher resource?

2. What are the noticeable differences between a Web resource and a Gopher resource?

FTP

4

CHAPTER

OBJECTIVES

Upon completing the material presented in this chapter, you should understand the following aspects of the Internet and using FTP:

◆ The concept behind File Transfer Protocol (FTP)
◆ How to retrieve a file with FTP using Netscape
◆ How to move among directories
◆ How to locate files
◆ How to transfer files
◆ How to identify file types
◆ How to use Archie to find files

WHY WOULD I WANT TO USE FTP?

Sometimes on the Internet all you want to do is to transfer a file from one place to another. This is where the **File Transfer Protocol**, or **FTP**, comes in. FTP has been around for as long as the Internet has existed. Remember, this was one of the original purposes in creating the Internet! Not only is FTP still used to transfer files from one big computer system to another, it is now being used by individual users to transfer files, say, from a server to the desktop computer.

FTP servers house a collection of files, whether they be digital copies of journals or texts, shareware or freeware software, or whatever. Users are able to connect to these servers, browse and locate a file they want, then *download,* or retrieve, a copy to the desktop computer. In fact, as you browse through the Web and the 'net, you will often see phrases like, "This software (or document) is available on the FTP server at . . . ."

FTP allows users to connect to a server in two ways: full-privilege and anonymous. Although FTP was originally designed to provide access to only the legitimate users of the machine (what is now called full-privilege FTP), when a need to come up with a scheme to make files available to the general public arose, anonymous FTP was devised. When you are accessing an FTP server via the Web, you are using anonymous FTP. You will find that there are some directories (folders) you cannot access—only certain folders on the FTP server are accessible by anonymous FTP users. Other folders appear empty when users open them.

FTP URL

As you locate a link on the Web, you might notice by the URL that it is an FTP server. An FTP URL has the format *ftp://server-name,* where *server-name* is the domain name of the FTP server. As with any other URL, you can connect to an FTP server via the Web by specifying its URL in the Location (Netsite) text box. You will also find that some FTP sites are fully developed web pages, containing intuitive graphics and other information. However, many of them offer little in the way of formatting.

BOX 4.1	**USING FTP TO OBTAIN SOFTWARE**

There are some large FTP archives of software available for you to explore. However, you will find by doing a Web search that many programs are available on regular Web servers.

Resource	URL
A huge software repository for many different computers.	ftp://wuarchive.wustl.edu
This archive site has a mirror of the Sim Tel archive, a large archive of MS-DOS programs. The original SimTel is no longer online.	ftp://oak.oakland.edu
The home of Info-Mac, another huge depository of Macintosh software.	ftp://sumex-aim.stanford.edu

Enter the URL **http://www.willamette.edu/~kpitter/esgtw.html**.

A screen similar to the one shown in Figure 4.1 is displayed.

Find the section "Chapter 4."

Position the mouse pointer over Netscape Communication's FTP site.

The URL displayed on the status message at the bottom is ftp://ftp.mcom.com/ indicating that this link connects you to the FTP server at Netscape.

Select the link.

An FTP screen similar to the one shown in Figure 4.2 is displayed.

NOTE: If the FTP site is unavailable or not a known host, Netscape will let you know. Usually the reason is that the site is too busy. However, make sure you typed the URL correctly.

THE FTP MENU

FTP servers organize files in a tree-like hierarchical file structure. There is a main menu (*root directory*) that displays a number of folders (*subdirectories*) and files. If you select a folder (subdirectory), another menu is displayed. Many FTP sites have a folder called "pub" that contains files that are accessible to anyone

FIGURE 4.1

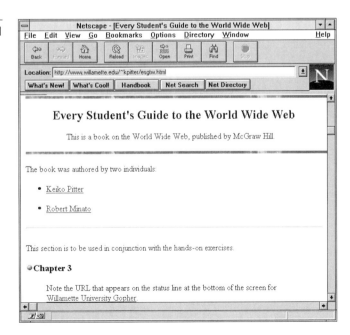

FIGURE 4.2

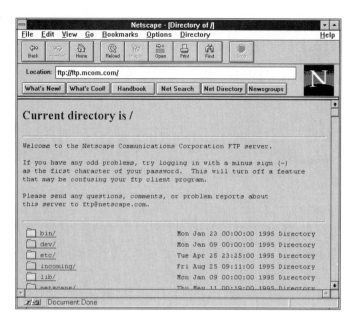

(anonymous FTP users). In fact, at some sites, the main menu displayed is already the pub menu.

MOVING AROUND

You move around within the FTP directories (folders) the same way you would follow links in any Web page. You can click on a link to select or go back one page.

NOTE: At some sites you may see the menu option ".." This is a DOS and UNIX convention. You can go back a page (or move up a directory level) by selecting it.

Select bin or incoming.

These folders appear empty. This is because you do not have "access" to these folders.

Go back one page.

Select pub to display the contents of this folder (directory).

Select one of the folders for Netscape and scroll down the page until you see a list of links, similar to the one shown in Figure 4.3.

The list includes text files and programs that can be downloaded. The different icons that appear in front of each menu item indicate the type of item displayed. Table 4-1 shows the symbols and their meanings.

FIGURE 4.3

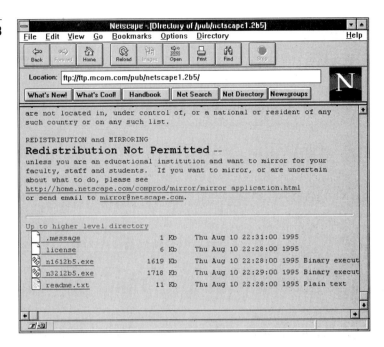

TABLE 4-1   FTP MENU ICONS

ICON	SELECTION TYPE	EXPLANATION
	Folder (subdirectory)	When you select this item, another menu is displayed.
	Document	An HTML, text, or PostScript file.
	File	A generic file. They might be compressed computer programs.
	Executable	An uncompressed program.

Once you locate a file you want, you can copy it to your local computer. A click of the mouse will begin this process, but it can get a bit confusing, as there may be many different kinds of files displayed in the same list and they are all displayed as links.

◆ If an item is a text file that can be displayed, select Save As from the File menu when the file is displayed. You can then specify where on your local computer you want to save this file.

◆ If an item is a file to be copied, a dialog box such as the one shown in Figure 4.4 is displayed. Click Save to Disk or Save Document, then specify where on your local computer you want this file saved.

FIGURE 4.4

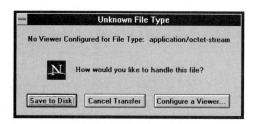

NOTE: For graphics or audio files, you might need helper applications, such as media players. Then you can click the Configure a Viewer button in the Unknown File Type dialog box to set up an application to play the file. If a viewer has already been configured, the file will either display, if it is text, or play, if it is a sound, video, or graphics file.

 Select readme.txt.

The file is displayed.

You can copy this file by selecting Save As from the File menu. Also, if you look at the URL, the location of a specific file is listed by giving the directory levels separated by a forward slash (/). For example, a file called readme.txt can be found on Netscape's FTP server by following the path /pub/netscape/windows/readme.txt.

 Go back one page.

Select an executable file for Netscape.

A dialog box is displayed.

If you wanted to copy this file, you would click on Save to Disk or Save Document. You won't do this now, however.

 Click on Cancel or Delete Document.

There you go! These basic functions—getting in, taking a look around, moving to where the file is, and getting back out again—are most of what you need to know to use FTP effectively. In fact, there's really only one other thing you need to know how to do, and that's how to find the files you want to retrieve.

NOTE: When you know the FTP server you want to access, you may want to use an FTP tool, rather than the Web, to retrieve the document or program. A popular FTP tool for the Mac platform is Fetch, and the one for Windows is WS_FTP.

ARCHIE: USER-INDEX OF ANONYMOUS FTP

As with any Web-accessible resource, you can use Web search tools to locate FTP sites—along with all other types of sites. However, there are some search tools for locating only FTP sites. One of the first, and still useful, tools to be developed was **Archie**. Archie's name is an abbreviation of the word "archives." Although it wasn't named after the comic book character, it has spawned a few imitators, the most famous being Veronica, which provides a similar service for Gopher.

What Archie provides is roughly analogous to the card catalog in the library, specifically, the catalog of titles. Archie accomplishes this feat by keeping track of nearly all of the anonymous FTP sites. Once a month or so, it searches these sites, compiling a list of all files. Then, once it has compiled its database, Archie is ready and waiting for queries from users.

Archie is based upon clients and servers. In this case, it is the server that searches FTP sites and maintains a huge database, and it is the client that asks the server to provide this information to the user.

USING ARCHIE

Here is the situation:

You're thinking of referring to *Alice in Wonderland* in a paper you're writing for your Abnormal Psychology class. What you need are some pithy quotes and speculative insight into the psyche of the author, to dress up your paper a bit.

It's just too bad that the nearest copy of *Alice in Wonderland* is over at the library, and you're in the computer center trying to work on your paper (and not about to give up your seat to one of those circling the lab for a parking space). However, you've heard that the Internet has all sorts of information online, so why not see what's out there about *Alice*? There's a good chance you can find the full text online, perhaps even the annotated version . . . maybe you can find out what Lewis Carroll was really talking about.

To check whether something worthwhile is available via FTP, you need to use Archie. There are a number of sites on the World Wide Web that include links to Archie servers.

 Enter the URL **http://pubweb.nexor.co.uk/public/archie/servers.html**.

A page similar to the one shown in Figure 4.5 is displayed, listing various Archie sites.

Choose a site by clicking. One from the continent you're living on makes sense, but it doesn't really matter; any site may be busy when you try to connect!

FIGURE 4.5

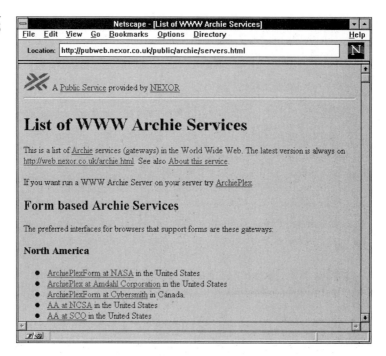

NOTE: The authors used ArosNet's Archie Gateway in North America for this example. Not all Archie services use the same interface; the first "box" to fill in is usually for your keyword, however.

A form will appear, indicating that Archie is ready to accept commands. The screen will be similar to the one shown in Figure 4.6.

This is a search based on the filename. That is, the search looks for the presence of keywords in the filename. The problem is that the titles of files on FTP sites are often less than descriptive. The titles you are looking for might range from "aliceinwonderland.hqx" to "theannotatedalice.zip." So rather than entering something like "alice," you will enter **alice. in. wonderland**, which should lead to results that are easier to interpret. The periods indicate an exact match for the phrase "alice in wonderland." Try seaching for "alice" later, and you'll see the obvious problem!

   In the Archie query: field, enter the following keywords: **alice. in. wonderland**. Click on the Search button.

Archie will search for all file titles containing the phrase "alice in wonderland." After a minute or two, a list will appear similar to the one shown in Figure 4.7.

FIGURE 4.6

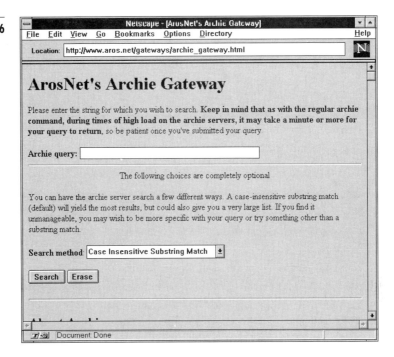

FIGURE 4.7

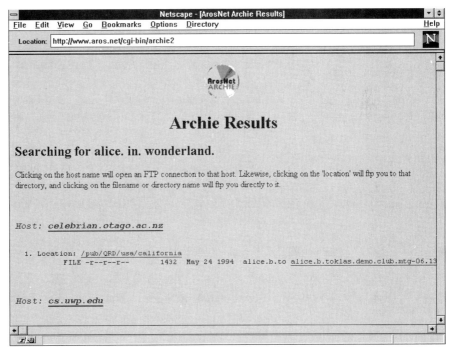

You can use the scroll bar to see the entire list. However, Netscape has a handy button to help you at the top of the screen. The Find button searches the current page for what you specify. Try searching for "carroll" and you should be able to locate the online text for Alice in Wonderland.

NOTE: These are some results obtained as this book was going to press. The results of your search may be dramatically different.

Let's look at some samples:

Host: **ftp.std.com**

1. **Location:** /obi/Lewis.Carroll/AliceInWonderl
   FILE -rw-rw-r--   1245   Jul 17 1990   alice.0 alice.0
2. **Location:** /obi/Lewis.Carroll/AliceInWonderl
   FILE -rw-rw-r--   11221   Jul 17 1990   alice.1 alice.1
3. **Location:** /obi/Lewis.Carroll/AliceInWonderl
   FILE -rw-rw-r--   11628   Jul 17 1990   alice.12 alice.12
4. **Location:** /obi/Lewis.Carroll/AliceInWonderl
   FILE -rw-rw-r--   10950   Jul 17 1990   alice.2 alice.2
5. **Location:** /obi/Lewis.Carroll/AliceInWonderl
   FILE -rw-rw-r--   9179   Jul 17 1990   alice.3 alice.3
6. **Location:** /obi/Lewis.Carroll/AliceInWonderl
   FILE -rw-rw-r--   13998   Jul 17 1990   alice.4 alice.4
7. **Location:** /obi/Lewis.Carroll/AliceInWonderl
   FILE -rw-rw-r--   11924   Jul 17 1990   alice.5 alice.5
8. **Location:** /obi/Lewis.Carroll/AliceInWonderl
   FILE -rw-rw-r--   13858   Jul 17 1990   alice.6 alice.6
9. **Location:** /obi/Lewis.Carroll/AliceInWonderl
   FILE -rw-rw-r--   12602   Jul 17 1990   alice.7 alice.7
10. **Location:** /obi/Lewis.Carroll/AliceInWonderl
   FILE -rw-rw-r--   37334   Jul 17 1990   alice.8 alice.8

Notice that the returned information is separated into sections, one for each server on which a match was found. The link to the "host" is the first item listed in each section. The *host* is the name of the FTP site on which the files are available. Below the link to the host, you'll see a link to the directory where the file is located. The next piece of information is the link to the file itself. There may be more than one file listed for each host, depending on what matched.

> *Host:* **cs.uwp.edu**
>
> **1. Location:** /pub/msdos/games/id/home-brew/levels/heretic/m-o
>   **FILE -rw-rw-r--   176876   May 18 02:58   malice.zi** malice.zip

Something to be aware of is ".zip" in filenames. This indicates a **compressed file**. Compression is a software process that shrinks the size of a file, making it easier to store and faster to transfer. Usually, a .zip file is for use by a machine running MS-DOS or Windows. You should remember that extension, though, when you're looking for MS-DOS or Windows files that aren't just text files. Compressed files need to be uncompressed after retrieval.

NOTE: You will find many compressed files on FTP. The reason is very simple: compressed files don't require as much storage space and are faster to transfer.

RETRIEVING A FILE

You will now retrieve the file from ftp.std.com.

 You can click on the site name, and locate the file at that site, or simply click on the filename to open or download the file immediately.

And there you are—all the tools you need to successfully use FTP to find and retrieve files from across the Internet.

SUMMARY

In this chapter many of the terms and concepts that are necessary to use FTP were introduced:

✦ The File Transfer Protocol (FTP) provides a way for files to be transferred between computers on the Internet.

✦ Netscape provides an easy way to retrieve files using FTP.

✦ In order to use FTP, you must know the address of the FTP server you want to access, or use one of the lists of FTP servers that can be found on the World Wide Web.

✦ There are two types of FTP: anonymous and full-privilege. Anonymous FTP allows users to access public files on the FTP server without having an account on that computer. For full-privilege FTP, you need an account.

◆ The files on an FTP server are organized in a hierarchical file structure. You need to know how to move through the directory structure in order to access files.

◆ The files retrieved using FTP are stored on your own computer.

◆ Archie is an index of anonymous FTP files, categorized by titles.

◆ Many of the files stored at FTP sites are in compressed format. These files must be uncompressed once retrieved.

KEY TERMS

anonymous FTP	compressed files	full-privilege FTP
Archie	File Transfer Protocol (FTP)	hierarchical file structure

REVIEW QUESTIONS

1. What is FTP?

2. How can you tell if a link leads to an FTP server?

3. What types of files can you transfer using FTP?

4. What is the difference between anonymous and full-privilege FTP?

5. On an FTP server, how can you tell if you have access to a folder (directory)?

6. When you retrieve a file using FTP, where does it get stored?

7. Explain how files are organized at an FTP site.

8. How do you move from one directory to another at an FTP site?

9. Once you have located a file, how do you retrieve it using Netscape?

10. What is the purpose of Archie?

EXERCISES

1. Find the FAQ for sci.physics. What is the URL of the server? Describe the location within the directory structure where the document was found.

2. Find the text of Edwin Abbott's *Flatland*. What is the URL of the server? Describe the location within the directory structure where the document was found.

3. How do you access the Smithsonian's collection of photographs? What categories of photographs are in its collection? How big is the collection? Specify how you discovered these things.

4. You've heard about an organization called the Free Software Foundation. (It names its software after wildebeests . . . that's good gnus!) The organization keeps a large FTP site somewhere that contains all the software it produces for public consumption. Where is this FTP site, and what kinds of programs can you get there?

DISCUSSION TOPICS

1. Do you think FTP as an Internet tool will continue to exist? Can FTP's function be replaced by the Web?

2. What are some of the limitations of Archie as a search tool?

TELNET

5 CHAPTER

OBJECTIVES

Upon completing the material presented in this chapter, you should understand the following aspects of the Internet and Telnet:

◆ The concept behind Telnet

◆ How to access Telnet sites

◆ How to use Telnet sites

◆ How to use Hytelnet

WHAT IS TELNET?

Telnet, one of the oldest tools on the Internet, allows you to log into a computer from a remote location, be it another computer at the same site or one across the country. Your own computer is being used as a dumb terminal. That is, during a Telnet session the real processing is done on the remote computer that you logged onto. The keystrokes from your keyboard are being accepted by the other computer, and your display is the output from the other computer.

WHY WOULD I USE TELNET?

There are still millions of Internet users who do not use the Web and are not planning to switch over any time soon. Hence, a considerable amount of information on the Internet is still in the textual world of Telnet—especially library catalogs. Although it is possible to start a Telnet session from Netscape by selecting a link to a Telnet resource or opening a Telnet URL, when you do, you are no longer using the World Wide Web. Netscape cannot conduct a Telnet session by itself, and instead must call on a Telnet program when a link calls for a Telnet session.

NOTE: You can specify which Telnet program to use and where it is located by displaying the Options menu and selecting the Preference option. See the appendix of this book for directions.

One of the most obvious changes when you start a Telnet session is the way in which the screen is displayed. You are no longer in a graphical interface, but in an old-fashioned text-based system. It may seem strange that Netscape, a program that manages to put almost every Internet resource in the same, graphical, click-and-point display, must use another program to display these Telnet resources.

But now, imagine for a moment what happens when you use a telephone—you pick up the receiver, enter a number, and are connected to another telephone. That phone will ring and be answered or give you a busy signal, or you might get a message saying that the number you have dialed is no longer in service. Telnet works much the same way, allowing you to "call" another machine, and interact with whatever (or whomever!) is on the other end.

A word of warning is necessary here: just like leaving home in the real world, traveling by Telnet is exciting, but you must leave the familiarity of your own environment behind—once you've logged onto another machine, you are at its mercy. The remote computer might display only text, not graphics, and the mouse on your computer might be usable only to cut and paste. The remote computer may offer user-friendly menus, or just a cryptic prompt awaiting your command. Nevertheless, by paying attention to what is happening on the screen and following clues for help and instructions, you can often successfully use remote computers. Even if the remote system doesn't provide much help, you should always be able to "hang up" on it.

A second word of warning: you cannot just Telnet to any computer system you see on the Internet. Some require that you have a valid user account on their system. Some will let you connect for a specific purpose only. For example, if you use the username "gopher," a computer at University of Minnesota named consultant.micro.umn.edu will let you connect to use the Gopher client. Still others will let you connect and display a general menu, such as the computer named techinfo.mit.edu at MIT.

TELNET URL

A Telnet URL has the format *telnet://domain-name:port/*, where domain-name is that of the computer you are trying to log onto. The *port*, which may or may not be specified, refers to a specific communication channel on which the destination computer is waiting for a request (similar to a phone extension). The default port number is 23. By entering a port number, you are overriding the default.

A TELNET SESSION

Rather than looking for a link that is Telnet, you will use an URL to connect to a Telnet site. Here is the scenario:

> You are reading the book *The Dharma Bums* by Jack Kerouac in your American Literature class. You enjoy this book and want to find out if he has written any other books. Unfortunately, your library doesn't have any other books by him in its collection. Also, you would like to write a critical paper on him as a person, and want to track down journal literature about him.

Many library catalogs and large bibliographic databases are available via Telnet for you to use. One such database is maintained by Data Research Associates, and you decide to start there. For the moment, let's just try to get on and off the system, and you will try the actual search later.

 In the Location (Netsite) text box, type **telnet://dra.com/**.

A Telnet session starts on your system. If the connection is successful, a session window similar to the one shown in Figure 5.1 is displayed.

If something happened and you didn't connect, check to make sure that you typed in the name correctly in the Location (Netsite) text box. If you see the message, "The domain name was invalid," most likely you have made a typing mistake. If you see the message, "Host or gateway not responding," it could mean that the remote machine is too busy to answer your call right now and that you should try again later. Sometimes names and addresses change with no warning, or a machine may be down, and you can't connect. This is a fact of life on the Internet, as it is with the telephone, and you have to look elsewhere for the information you seek. For the moment, let's assume that you have connected successfully.

FIGURE 5.1

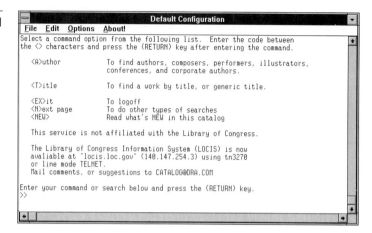

As you can see in Figure 5.1, this system gives you a menu option to disconnect (<EX>it). However, there are many systems for which ways to disconnect are not so obvious. If you can type a command, one of the following commands may disconnect you: **logoff**, **logout**, **quit**, **bye**, **exit**. If none of this works, you always have the option to quit the Telnet program. If you need to quit the program, open the File menu and select Exit.

If you are successful at disconnecting from the remote computer, the Telnet window will close.

 Type ex and press ENTER.

The session window disappears and you return to the Web screen.

BOX 5.1 | ## IS ANYBODY HOME?

Sometimes you cannot Telnet to a site that you visited yesterday. There are a number of possible causes for this quirk, including:

✦ The Telnet client is unable to find the requested machine, either because its address was entered incorrectly or because it doesn't exist.

✦ The remote computer is powered off.

✦ The remote computer is refusing to connect to your machine.

✦ A computer network is down.

These are usually temporary problems. If the problem persists for more than a day, you may want to contact your local computer support staff to see if they can determine the cause. If you have the same problem with a number of different machines, you may want to contact your local computer support staff to make sure the problem is not occurring at your local site.

Now that you've successfully connected to and disconnected from a system, let's try searching that system. When connecting to remote databases, you must at least read the screens presented to you to be able to use the database. You may also find it useful to read the available Help information. Some systems are easier to use than others, but it is always wise to read any information you can about the system when using it.

 Connect to the dra.com database again using the same method as before.

You are looking for more books by Jack Kerouac.

 Type **A** for an Author Search and press (ENTER).

The Author Search screen, similar to the one shown in Figure 5.2, is displayed.

You are now presented with a screen and several examples. This is why it is important to read the screen when connecting to remote systems. Although you may have never used the system before, you can often determine what to do next by looking at the screen. In this case, to find books by Jack Kerouac, type **Kerouac, Jack** at the Enter Author prompt.

NOTE: If you make a mistake while typing, just backspace and correct your entry. If you end up somewhere you didn't intend, typing **st** should return you to the main menu.

 Type **Kerouac, Jack** and press (ENTER).

A screen similar to the one shown in Figure 5.3 is displayed.

FIGURE 5.2

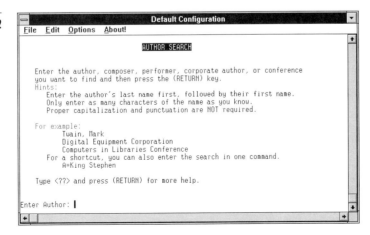

FIGURE 5.3

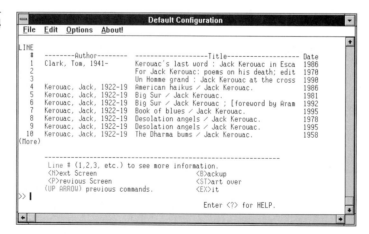

```
┌─────────────────────────────────────────────────────────────────────┐
│ ═                           Default Configuration                   ▼ │
│  File   Edit   Options   About!                                       │
│ ┌───────────────────────────────────────────────────────────────┬─┐ │
│ │LINE   # of                                                     │▲│ │
│ │  #   titles   --------------------------- Authors ------------│ │ │
│ │  1     49    Kerouac, Jack, 1922-1969.                         │ │ │
│ │  2      1    Kerouac, Jack, 1922-1969. Brothers.               │ │ │
│ │  3      1    Kerouac, Jack, 1922-1969. Correspondence. Selections. │ │
│ │  4      1    Kerouac, Jack, 1922-1969. On the road.            │ │ │
│ │  5      1    Kerouac, Jack, 1922-1969. Pic. 1988.              │ │ │
│ │  6      2    Kerouac, Jack, 1922-1969. Poems. Selections.      │ │ │
│ │  7      1    Kerouac, Jack, 1922-1969. Satori in Paris.        │ │ │
│ │  8      1    Kerouac, Jack, 1922-1969. Veille de Noel. 1973.   │ │ │
│ │                                                                │ │ │
│ │                                                                │ │ │
│ │              -----------------------------------------------   │ │ │
│ │Enter:  Line #   (1,2,3, etc.) to see works associated with your search. │
│ │        <N>ext screen                          <B>ackup         │ │ │
│ │        <P>revious screen                      <ST>art over     │ │ │
│ │        <LIM>it search                         <EX>it           │ │ │
│ │>>                                                              │ │ │
│ │                                        Enter <?> for HELP.     │▼│ │
│ └───────────────────────────────────────────────────────────────┴─┘ │
│ ←                                                                   → │
└─────────────────────────────────────────────────────────────────────┘
```

This screen displays several sets of books with the number of titles contained within each set. The first set, for example, contains 49 titles. To display the set, enter the line number. Right now, you want to see the first set.

Type 1 and press ENTER.

A list similar to the one shown in Figure 5.4 is displayed.

You can see that Kerouac has written many books, and now you can decide whether you want to try to obtain one of these books through your local library or bookstore.

Now that you've found your way into the system, can you find your way back out? You have found the information which you sought, and you need to disconnect from the session. Fortunately, there is a Disconnect menu option

FIGURE 5.4

```
┌─────────────────────────────────────────────────────────────────────┐
│ ═                           Default Configuration                   ▼ │
│  File   Edit   Options   About!                                       │
│ ┌───────────────────────────────────────────────────────────────┬─┐ │
│ │LINE                                                            │▲│ │
│ │  #    --------Author--------   ---------------Title----------- Date │
│ │  1   Clark, Tom, 1941-        Kerouac's last word : Jack Kerouac in Esca 1986 │
│ │  2                            For Jack Kerouac: poems on his death; edit 1970 │
│ │  3                            Un Homme grand : Jack Kerouac at the cross 1990 │
│ │  4   Kerouac, Jack, 1922-19   American haikus / Jack Kerouac.  1986 │
│ │  5   Kerouac, Jack, 1922-19   Big Sur / Jack Kerouac.          1981 │
│ │  6   Kerouac, Jack, 1922-19   Big Sur / Jack Kerouac ; [foreword by Aram 1992 │
│ │  7   Kerouac, Jack, 1922-19   Book of blues / Jack Kerouac.    1995 │
│ │  8   Kerouac, Jack, 1922-19   Desolation angels / Jack Kerouac. 1978 │
│ │  9   Kerouac, Jack, 1922-19   Desolation angels / Jack Kerouac. 1995 │
│ │ 10   Kerouac, Jack, 1922-19   The Dharma bums / Jack Kerouac.  1958 │
│ │(More)                                                          │ │ │
│ │              -----------------------------------------------   │ │ │
│ │        Line # (1,2,3, etc.) to see more information.           │ │ │
│ │        <N>ext Screen                          <B>ackup         │ │ │
│ │        <P>revious Screen                      <ST>art over     │ │ │
│ │        (UP ARROW) previous commands.          <EX>it           │ │ │
│ │>> |                                                            │ │ │
│ │                                        Enter <?> for HELP.     │▼│ │
│ └───────────────────────────────────────────────────────────────┴─┘ │
│ ←                                                                   → │
└─────────────────────────────────────────────────────────────────────┘
```

on screen. If, however, you don't see any obvious way to disconnect, you can try the following:

 Type **help** or **?** and see if anything happens. In this case, the **??** command gives you help on searching the database.

Try typing **bye**, **exit**, **quit**, or **logoff**.

Type **ex** and press ENTER.

The session window will close.

USERNAMES AND TERMINAL EMULATION

As you have seen in this session, remote machines can sometimes give you very clear instructions; at other times they can be complex and confusing. Always take a look around for any help or ? commands that you can use to obtain further instructions on how to navigate the system to which you have connected.

You probably didn't notice, but in the session you just completed several details were taken care of automatically. While this is nice, it doesn't always happen that way. Two such details were logging in with a **username** and selecting a terminal emulation. Often, when you connect to a remote machine, you will be greeted by a not-so-friendly prompt: login:. Sometimes you will know the correct way to *login*, and sometimes you won't. Sometimes you can guess the login name to use, because it will closely match the service you are trying to reach. For example, if you are trying to reach a library catalog, try typing the login name "library," or if you are trying to Telnet to a Gopher, try logging in as "gopher." You can often find a login name in the same place that you found the address. Beware, though: some systems also require a password or may be restricted so that outside users cannot access them without an account. If you know the correct login name and still are prompted for a password, check to make sure that you have entered the login name correctly. On many systems, "LIBRARY" and "library" are considered different—that is, it matters whether you type text in upper- or lowercase characters. In most instances, lowercase is preferred.

You may now be wondering how you can find the address and login information of machines that might interest you. When you select a Telnet resource on a Web page, a dialog box will pop up to give login information such as, "Use the account name 'brsuser' to log in."

The other question you are often asked upon logging in is to identify your terminal type, or your **terminal emulation**. Just as with a telephone, you can end up calling someone who doesn't speak your language. The other party's response will appear as garbled characters on the screen. Fortunately, many systems offer you a choice of terminal types. You may be presented with

```
What kind of Terminal are you using?
      V > VT100
      W > WYSE emulating TVI925
      A > CCCII PC
      B > HEATHKIT H19
      C > TANDEM
      D > TVI910
      E > TVI920
      F > TVI925
```

Most Telnet software emulates vt100 or vt220. If, upon choosing those options, strange things happen, you may have a different type of terminal emulation. Ask your instructor or system administrator for help.

HYTELNET: WHERE'S THE PHONE BOOK?

We've talked now a bit about how you can use Telnet, but we haven't told you where you can find addresses. When you conduct a Net Search, some of the resources located could be Telnet sites. However, there is someone out there on the Internet who has taken charge of compiling a vast database of Telnet addresses, including the addresses of most of the Internet-accessible library catalogs. This database, compiled by Peter Scott of the University of Saskatchewan, is called **Hytelnet.** You can access it over—what else?—the World Wide Web.

Although Hytelnet is not a comprehensive list of every Telnet site address on the Internet, it is a very good place to get an idea of the types of information and resources available. The database is frequently updated as new services become available.

Let's connect to the Hytelnet database and see what types of resources are available:

 In the Location (Netsite) text box, enter **http://www.usask.ca/cgi-bin/ hytelnet.**

A screen similar to the one shown in Figure 5.5 is displayed.

You are now using the Hytelnet program using the Web. Take a minute to read the screen to see what types of information are available. Since we have already looked at a library catalog, let's select Other Resources.

FIGURE 5.5

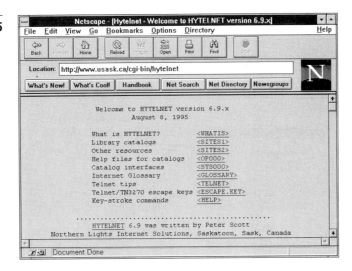

Select Other Resources by clicking on <SITE2>.

A screen similar to Figure 5.6 is displayed.

As you can see, many types of resources are available via Telnet, including resources listed in other chapters of this book. As we are interested in literature, English literature in particular, let's choose the Databases and bibliographies option.

Select Databases and bibliographies by clicking on <FUL 000>.

A screen similar to Figure 5.7 is displayed.

FIGURE 5.6

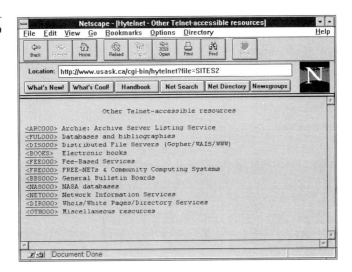

FIGURE 5.7

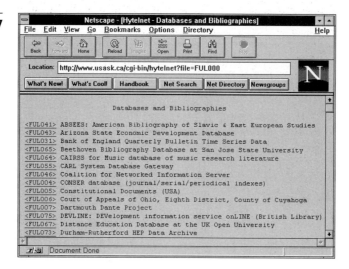

Notice that this menu contains many items, covering diverse topics. Take a moment to scroll through the menu.

In our quest for journal literature on Jack Kerouac, let's take a look at CARL System Database Gateway.

   Select CARL System Database Gateway by clicking on <FUL055>.

You should see a menu similar to the one shown in Figure 5.8.

The document tells you that you can access CARL by Telnetting to "database.carl.org" or "192.54.81.76" and selecting vt100 as the terminal type. All you

FIGURE 5.8

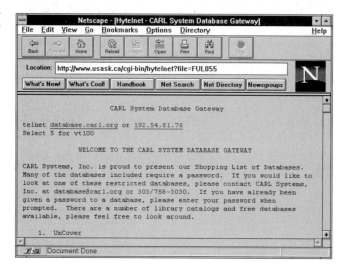

need to do to start a Telnet session is to select the link on the current Web page or type the URL, **telnet://database.carl.org/**, in the Location text box.

Start a Telnet session to database.carl.org using whichever method you prefer.

A screen similar to the one shown in Figure 5.9 is displayed.

Type **5** and press ENTER to select VT100 as the terminal type.

You should see a screen similar to the one shown in Figure 5.10

This is the opening screen for the system at CARL (The Colorado Alliance of Research Libraries). The message on screen describes restrictions and costs involved in using this service. It also tells you that if you want to leave at any time, type **//EXIT**. You want to use the UnCover option which is an open-access (free) journal article index with fee-based full-text delivery options.

FIGURE 5.9

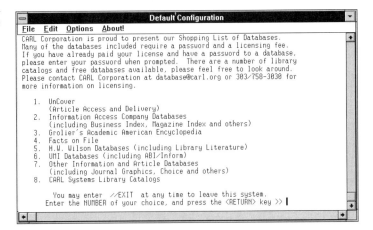

```
Default Configuration
File  Edit  Options  About!
Trying 8021040076...Open
Welcome to the CARL system
Please identify your terminal. Choices are:
1.ADM (all)
2.APPLE,IBM
3.TANDEM
4.TELE-914
5.VT100
6.WYSE 50
7.ZENTEC
8.HARDCOPY
9.IBM 316x
Use HARDCOPY if your terminal type isn't listed..
SELECT LINE #: |
```

FIGURE 5.10

```
Default Configuration
File  Edit  Options  About!
CARL Corporation is proud to present our Shopping List of Databases.
Many of the databases included require a password and a licensing fee.
If you have already paid your license and have a password to a database,
please enter your password when prompted.  There are a number of library
catalogs and free databases available, please feel free to look around.
Please contact CARL Corporation at database@carl.org or 303/758-3030 for
more information on licensing.

   1.  UnCover
       (Article Access and Delivery)
   2.  Information Access Company Databases
       (including Business Index, Magazine Index and others)
   3.  Grolier's Academic American Encyclopedia
   4.  Facts on File
   5.  H.W. Wilson Databases (including Library Literature)
   6.  UMI Databases (including ABI/Inform)
   7.  Other Information and Article Databases
       (including Journal Graphics, Choice and others)
   8.  CARL Systems Library Catalogs

       You may enter  //EXIT  at any time to leave this system.
       Enter the NUMBER of your choice, and press the <RETURN> key >> |
```

Type **1** and press ENTER.

For the next three screens, you are informed of the access options for UnCover. You just want to browse through for now, so you can ignore these.

 Press ENTER several times, until you reach an UnCover welcome message similar to the one shown in Figure 5.11.

As with many remote systems, it is hard to guess how to search this one without reading the Help screen. You can take a moment to read it, or just give it a try. Here you are going to do a Word search, since you want articles about Jack Kerouac. (If you use Author Search here you will retrieve articles *by* Jack Kerouac, not *about* him.)

 Type **W** and press ENTER.

A screen similar to Figure 5.12 is displayed.

FIGURE 5.11

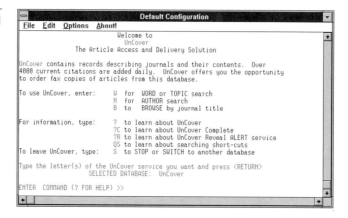

FIGURE 5.12

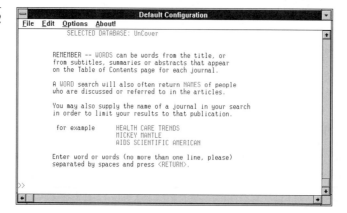

Again, the instructions on screen tell you how to enter words for searching.

Type Jack Kerouac and press (ENTER).

A screen similar to Figure 5.13 is displayed.

You should now see the number of citations retrieved. You are also asked whether you wish to enter a new word or display what you've retrieved. You will display the list of titles.

Type D and press (ENTER).

A list of articles similar to the one in Figure 5.14 is displayed.

You should now see a list of titles of journal articles and the names and dates of the journals in which the articles appeared. You can see the rest of the list by pressing (ENTER).

FIGURE 5.13

```
┌─────────────────────────────────────────────────────────────┐
│  ─                    Default Configuration              ▼   │
│  File  Edit  Options  About!                                 │
│ ┌──────────────────────────────────────────────────────┬─┐ │
│ │ WORKING...                                            │▲│ │
│ │ JACK  1600 ITEMS       UnCover                        │ │ │
│ │ JACK + KEROUAC     11 ITEMS                           │ │ │
│ │                                                       │ │ │
│ │ JACK + KEROUAC     11 ITEMS  UnCover                  │ │ │
│ │                                                       │ │ │
│ │ You may make your search more specific  (and reduce   │ │ │
│ │ the size of the list)  by adding another word         │ │ │
│ │ to your search. The result will be items in           │ │ │
│ │ your current list that also contain the new           │ │ │
│ │ word.                                                 │ │ │
│ │                                                       │ │ │
│ │  to ADD a new word, enter it,                         │ │ │
│ │                                                       │ │ │
│ │  <D>ISPLAY to see the current list, or                │ │ │
│ │                                                       │ │ │
│ │  <Q>UIT for a new search:                             │ │ │
│ │                                                       │ │ │
│ │ NEW WORD(S): │                                        │▼│ │
│ │ ◄                                                     ►│ │ │
│ └──────────────────────────────────────────────────────┴─┘ │
└─────────────────────────────────────────────────────────────┘
```

FIGURE 5.14

```
┌─────────────────────────────────────────────────────────────┐
│  ─                    Default Configuration              ▼   │
│  File  Edit  Options  About!                                 │
│ ┌──────────────────────────────────────────────────────┬─┐ │
│ │ 2 Gifford, Barry              (California journal. 01/01/95)│ │
│ │    The dream factory.                                 │ │ │
│ │                                                       │ │ │
│ │ 3 Stevens, Jay                      (Yankee. 09/01/94)│ │ │
│ │    Classic Jack.                                      │ │ │
│ │                                                       │ │ │
│ │ 4               (ABM, Australian business monthly. 03/01/94)│ │
│ │    And the beat goes on.                              │ │ │
│ │                                                       │ │ │
│ │ 5                       (The Missouri review. 1994  ) │ │ │
│ │    Found Text Series--Jack Kerouac.                   │ │ │
│ │                                                       │ │ │
│ │ 6 Robertson, David      (Western american literature. Fall 92 )│ │
│ │    Real Matter, Spiritual Mountain: Gary Snyder and Jac...│ │
│ │                                                       │ │ │
│ │ 7 Mansfield, Howard            (New letters. Wint 92 )│ │ │
│ │    On the Eulogy Road: Claiming Jack Kerouac.         │ │ │
│ │                                                       │ │ │
│ │ <RETURN> to CONTINUE, Number + M (ex. 3M)to MARK article│ │
│ │ Enter <Line numbers> to see FULL records             │ │ │
│ │ <P>revious for PREVIOUS page,<Q>uit for NEW search    │▼│ │
│ │ ◄                                                     ►│ │ │
│ └──────────────────────────────────────────────────────┴─┘ │
└─────────────────────────────────────────────────────────────┘
```

FIGURE 5.15

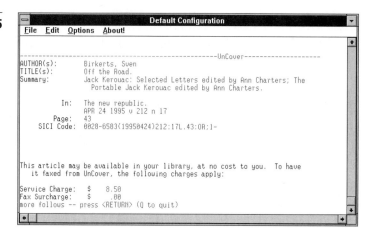

```
-------------------------------------------------UnCover-------------------
AUTHOR(s):      Birkerts, Sven
TITLE(s):       Off the Road.
Summary:        Jack Kerouac: Selected Letters edited by Ann Charters; The
                Portable Jack Kerouac edited by Ann Charters.

        In:     The new republic.
                APR 24 1995 v 212 n 17
      Page:     43
  SICI Code:    0028-6583(19950424)212:17L.43:OR;1-



This article may be available in your library, at no cost to you.  To have
  it faxed from UnCover, the following charges apply:

Service Charge:   $    8.50
Fax Surcharge:    $     .00
more follows -- press <RETURN> (Q to quit)
```

 Press ⌈ENTER⌋.

Notice that the articles are listed in reverse chronological order. You may want to take note of when articles began appearing in this database. Often online information does not cover older material. You may want to check print indexes for older resources. Selecting a line number will display the full citation of an article. Select an article that looks interesting to you, say, 1.

 Type **1** and press ⌈ENTER⌋.

More detailed information is shown, similar to that displayed in Figure 5.15.

This gives you the information you need to get the article from your library, or if you'd rather purchase the article from CARL, that information is also given.

It's time to leave this database. As you recall, the instructions on screen told you to type **//EXIT** to leave the system. Why don't you try doing this part on your own!

 Exit the database. This should end the Telnet session.

SUMMARY

In this chapter, many of the terms and concepts necessary to use Telnet are introduced:

✦ Telnet allows you to connect directly to another computer system.

✦ When you Telnet to another system, you have to learn the commands for that computer system. Some systems require that you have an account.

✦ A Telnet URL has the format *telnet://domain-name:port/*.

✦ If you get stuck in another computer, quit from the Telnet program by pulling down the File menu and selecting Exit or Quit.

✦ Some systems will require that you specify the terminal type (or "emulation"). Most likely, you are using vt100.

✦ The Hytelnet database is a compilation of many useful Telnet addresses.

KEY TERMS

Hytelnet	terminal emulation	username
Telnet		

REVIEW QUESTIONS

1. Why would you want to use Telnet sites?

2. How can you tell if an URL is for Telnet?

3. Say that you selected a link for a Telnet from a Web page, but it didn't work. What could be the problem?

4. Do you need an account on the computer to which you connect?

5. If you get stuck while connected to another computer system, what can you do?

6. What is terminal emulation?

7. What is Hytelnet?

EXERCISES

1. Using Hytelnet, find the library nearest you whose catalog is accessible via the Internet. What is the URL of the site you chose? Connect to that catalog, then locate and describe what books it has on the subject of United States history.

2. Suppose you are reading William Faulkner's *The Sound and the Fury* in your English class, and you are wondering if William Faulkner has written any other books, or if anyone has written books about him. Using Hytelnet, find three books by or about William Faulkner. What are the titles?

3. Access the Telnet site telnet://database.carl.org/. This service offers many databases, some of which are fee-based, and some of which are free. You should be able to get to the main menu just by pressing [ENTER] in response to the numerous questions asked. Locate the menu option CARL Uncover. Use this database to determine whether any recent magazine articles have been published about mental illness among the homeless. List the magazines and article titles. Hint: Use the "W" Word Search function.

4. Access the Telnet site telnet://sjsulib1.sjsu.edu/. From the main menu displayed, select "d," then "Beethoven Bibliography Database." Search this database to identify works that deal with Beethoven's deafness. Also, see if you can find any works that compare Beethoven to Schumann. Describe what you found.

5. Access the Telnet site at the Library of Congress, telnet://locis.loc.gov/. Determine whether there has been any recent legislation regarding the National Information Infostructure. Describe what you found. (Hint: You will not find this in the Library of Congress catalog.)

DISCUSSION TOPICS

1. What are some of the difficulties you may run into using Telnet sites?

2. Why do we need to use Telnet sites?

E-MAIL

6

CHAPTER

OBJECTIVES

Upon completing the material in this chapter, you should understand the following aspects of the Internet and e-mail:

◆ The concept behind e-mail (electronic mail)

◆ The limitations of Web e-mail

◆ How to send a message from an e-mail URL

◆ How to send a message by selecting a command

◆ Effective use of e-mail

◆ How to use the e-mail feature of Netscape Navigator 2.0

WHAT IS E-MAIL?

E-mail (electronic mail) is a system for sending messages or files to the accounts of other computer users. The senders and recipient(s) may be on the same or different computer systems. E-mail works very much like regular postal mail. Every user on the network has a private mailbox. In order to send someone a message, you need to know his or her address and how to compose and send the message using mail software. To read e-mail, you also need to know how to

BOX 6.1	**POP MAIL SERVERS**

Consider the following problem: You and the other 100 people in your dorm each have a network connection in your room. Each of you has a PC running Windows or a Macintosh, and all of them are connected to the Internet, so you can use client software.

But what happens if you want to send each other mail? To send mail directly to each other's PC or Macintosh, you'll have to know the names of the machines: would Jack Mullen's address be "jmullen@room206.metanoia-hall.unseen.edu" or just "jmullen@futon.unseen.edu"? And what if a machine is turned off when someone is trying to send mail? For these reasons and more, your group needs something called a **Post Office Protocol (POP) mail server**.

The POP mail server is installed on a centralized machine on campus. It is always on, and it provides the same address ("unseen.edu," perhaps) for everyone. Your mail goes to this machine and stays there. Then, when you are ready to read it on your own machine, the POP mail client software on your computer can ask the server to send it to you.

This has certain advantages, the foremost being that you can now use the familiar Microsoft Windows or Macintosh point-and-click interface to read and answer your e-mail. But there is one significant drawback that has to do with the e-mail messages that are on the POP mail server after you've read them. Most POP mail clients give you options of either deleting them or leaving copies on the POP server. Both options present a problem.

If you delete them, the only copies of your e-mail are now on your computer's hard drive. Why is this bad? Well, as long as you read your e-mail from only one machine, this is not bad. In fact, it's pretty good, because you don't have to go across a network to retrieve your e-mail. But you can't use this in a lab, for instance, because all of your e-mail will now be on the lab machine, and you can't transfer it back to the POP mail server. You have to read and delete all of it from the machine you are currently using.

If you leave the mail there, then you have to periodically get on the host machine (and use its mail reading program) to delete your accumulated messages. In fact, with some POP mail client programs, each time you access the POP server, all the accumulated mail is transferred to your computer in its entirety over and over again. You can end up with multiple copies of the same mail on your computer.

use mail software. In addition, you will want to know how to *archive* (save), delete, and reply to messages you receive.

Most Web browsers can do some of the e-mail functions. Some require that you specify a valid e-mail address for the sender field; others do not. Netscape versions previous to Navigator 2.0 let you send e-mail, provided you specify an e-mail address in the Preference box. Starting with Navigator 2.0, it also lets you read e-mail messages that you receive at the address specified during setup. The Netscape mail reader is a POP mail program; it works in conjunction with the POP mail server installed on the Internet host computer where you have an account. When e-mail messages are delivered to the host computer, the POP server transfers them to the Netscape mail reader on your computer.

NOTE: Look at the appendix for directions for entering e-mail addresses through Mail and News in the Options menu.

The Mac and Windows versions of the Netscape mail feature have slightly different screens, and some of the field names, icons, and column headings are different. Screens displayed here are for the Windows version.

NOTE: At the time of this writing, Netscape Release 2 beta was having considerable problems with e-mail. Therefore, coverage of reading e-mail is kept to a minimum in this text.

SENDING E-MAIL MESSAGES

There are two ways in which you might send an e-mail from Netscape. One is to select a link that is an e-mail URL. The other is to create an e-mail message from a command option.

E-MAIL URL

An e-mail URL lets you send a message to a particular person. It has the format "mailto:*user-address*," where *user-address* is the complete e-mail **address** of the person to whom you can *send* an e-mail message. One thing that's different from other URLs is that you do not enter this in the Location (Netsite) text box. Rather, if you see a link with the URL in this format, you know the mail will be sent to the person specified. Web authors often put an e-mail URL in a Web page so they can get comments or responses from people who have accessed their Web page. Let's try one.

 Open the URL by typing **http://www.willamette.edu/~kpitter/ esgtw.html**.

A screen similar to the one shown in Figure 6.1 is displayed.

FIGURE 6.1

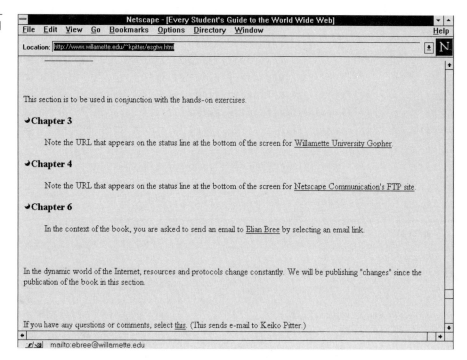

```
   Netscape - [Every Student's Guide to the World Wide Web]
File   Edit   View   Go   Bookmarks   Options   Directory   Window                        Help

Location: http://www.willamette.edu/~kpitter/esgtw.html                                    N

This section is to be used in conjunction with the hands-on exercises.

Chapter 3
    Note the URL that appears on the status line at the bottom of the screen for Willamette University Gopher.

Chapter 4
    Note the URL that appears on the status line at the bottom of the screen for Netscape Communication's FTP site.

Chapter 6
    In the context of the book, you are asked to send an email to Elian Bree by selecting an email link.

In the dynamic world of the Internet, resources and protocols change constantly. We will be publishing "changes" since the
publication of the book in this section.

If you have any questions or comments, select this. (This sends e-mail to Keiko Pitter.)

      mailto:ebree@willamette.edu
```

Halfway down the screen is a section called "Chapter 6."

 Position the mouse pointer over "Elian Bree."

The URL displayed on the status line at the bottom is mailto:ebree@willamette.edu.

By selecting this link, you can send an e-mail to Elian Bree, whose e-mail address is ebree@willamette.edu.

 Click on "Elian Bree."

A Mail Document dialog box similar to the one shown in Figure 6.2 is displayed.

ANATOMY OF AN E-MAIL MESSAGE

An e-mail message has two parts: the header and the body. The header has information about the message, such as to whom the message is sent, who the message is from, and what the subject of the message is. The header may also contain other information, such as the time when the message was sent. The body, on the other hand, is the text of the message itself. Be aware of these two parts, because when you send e-mail, you'll need to put information in both places.

FIGURE 6.2

Netscape - [ebree@willamette.edu]

File   Edit   View   Window

| Send | Quote Doc << | | Attach | | |

From: Calvin Brown <brownc@willamette.edu>
Send To: ebree@willamette.edu
Subject:
Attachment:

COMPOSING AND SENDING A MESSAGE

Looking at Figure 6.2, you can see that both the From and To fields already contain addresses.

Click the mouse to move the cursor to the Subject field.

Type **Introduction** in this field.

Now position the cursor in the message field, and type the body of the message. Introduce yourself to Elian.

Notice the Quote Doc (Windows) or Quote (Mac) button. If you want to include the text of the current Web page in your message (let's say that you are sending comments about the Web page you are viewing), you can do so by pressing this button. You can then edit the quoted text to include just the section you want.

At this point, you can either send the message or cancel it.

Click on the Send button.

The message has been sent to Elian. If you check your e-mail account later, you will notice that Elian sent you a reply.

Another way to send a message is by selecting commands on the menu. In the older versions of Netscape (and still supported in Release 2), the command is given from the File menu.

From the File menu, select New Mail Message.

The Mail Document dialog box is displayed. This time, however, the To field has not been filled.

To send a message, simply fill in the recipient's e-mail address in the To field. You know how to do the rest.

NOTE: You can send another message to Elian, but you will receive exactly the same message back from her. You will find to your dismay that—as nice an entity as Elian is—she is only a computer program that returns automatic replies. So any conversation with Elian may be a bit one-sided!

 From the File menu, select Close to return to the Web browser.

FINDING E-MAIL ADDRESSES

The best way to find someone's e-mail address is to ask the person. There is not yet a foolproof way to find a person's e-mail address on the Internet. Many people now list their e-mail addresses along with their postal mail address on business cards and in other directories.

If you at least know the name of the user's institution, you can connect to the Web page and see if there is a directory. You can also try the Internet white pages

---

BOX 6.2

HOW TO SEND E-MAIL TO ANOTHER NETWORK MAIL SYSTEM

Other Network	Address on the Other Network	Internet Address
America Online	\<user>	\<user>@aol.com
AppleLink	\<id>	\<id>@applelink.apple.com
BITNET	\<user>@\<node>	\<user>@\<node>.bitnet
CompuServ	71234,567	71234.567@compuserv.com
Fidonet	john smith at 1:2/3.4	john.smith@p4.f3.n2.z1. fidonet.org
MCIMail	John Smith (123-4567)	1234567@mcimail.com JSmith@mcimail.com John_Smith@mcimail.com
SprintMail	John Smith at SomeOrg	SomeOrg/G=John/S=Smth/ O=SomeOrg /ADMD= TELEMAIL/C=US/ @sprint.com

(http://home.mcom.com/home/internet-white-pages.html). Just make sure to read the instructions on the screen before attempting to use this service.

EFFECTIVE USE OF E-MAIL

To some, e-mail appears to be just a faster way of delivering letters. Others think of it as a substitute for telephone communication: Messages can often be sent and replied to within minutes. However, e-mail is a mode of communication that is different from both postal and telephone systems, with its own advantages and drawbacks. Ironically, some of the advantages are also drawbacks.

E-mail gets a message from one point to another very quickly and, at least to the user, it is often much cheaper than a telephone for instant long-distance communication. Furthermore, the sender can send it when it's convenient and the recipient can likewise read it when it's convenient. However, this also means that no matter how quickly a message may arrive at its destination, it may be "late" if the receiver fails to check his or her e-mail on a regular basis.

E-mail certainly makes it easy to distribute messages to multiple receivers, but because it is so easy, junk mail is sent to a large number of people. For instance, chain letters can flood the network and take up storage on the recipient's host computer. Remember, e-mail is not removed until the recipient deletes it.

E-mail is ideal for informal discussions and quick responses. However, it is a *written* form of communication, so individuals are more accountable for what they write than with spoken communication. Many people tend to drift into informality in their messages and do not spend the time needed to construct a formal message. Furthermore, your messages might be saved by those who receive them, and they might later hold you accountable for rash words. They may even forward it on to others, to your potential embarrassment.

On the Internet, one person's e-mail message looks just like another, and often conveys little information about that person. Age, nationality, sex, or other factors that may influence face-to-face communication are not immediately apparent. Sometimes users forget that there really is a living person at the other end. Messages can become informal, impersonal, or curt, or, at the other extreme, too personal or involved. All the etiquette one may practice in face-to-face or even standard written communication may be forgotten or become secondary in electronic communication, and careless comments can lead to misunderstanding or ill feelings.

Also, security is low in e-mail communication. You should never send any e-mail message that you wouldn't want to become public knowledge—because it might! Finally, you should be aware that it is possible—and not very difficult—to "forge" e-mail, especially in Netscape. So, if you get a message from someone

BOX 6.3

MAKING FACES

Because in e-mail it is difficult to add tone and context to messages, users on the Internet have adopted some conventions to signal that they are making jokes or speaking lightheartedly. Some people will put remarks in <> brackets. For example, they might write "That was an awful party <hee hee>" or <grin> or just <g>. Also some users draw pictures of smiling or winking faces, called "smilies" or "emoticons."

Here are some examples. Note that you have to look at these pictures sideways—the colon or semicolon forms the eyes.

  :)   happy
  :(sad
  ;)   wink
  :P   sticking tongue out

Some faces can get rather complicated. Use your imagination!

---

that seems out of character, check with the sender before replying with an attack. He or she may not have sent the message, and you may be the victim of a malicious prank!

After you use e-mail for a while, you'll see a lot of messages that obviously should never have been sent and that the sender no doubt regrets. To prevent making such mistakes yourself, here are some guidelines:

✦ Never send an e-mail message that you wouldn't want to become public knowledge.

✦ Keep the length of each line reasonable (fewer than 60 characters) to make sure that each line is viewable from any terminal. Displayed line length is different depending on the terminal and the software being used, and sometimes this results in text being chopped off.

✦ Don't send abusive, harassing, or bigoted messages.

✦ Senders may approach e-mail as a medium for friendly, informal conversation, but recipients frequently view the messages much more seriously than they were intended. You can't control how the receiver will perceive your message; so be careful.

✦ Use both upper- and lowercase characters. Messages written in all uppercase are perceived to be harsh, like shouting. All lowercase is too informal at times.

✦ Be careful with sarcasm or jokes. Readers cannot see your facial expressions or hear the tone of your voice.

✦ When responding to a message with multiple recipients, be very careful to whom you are responding. Usually there is an option to either respond to the sender alone or to also respond to all the recipients listed. You do not want to be embarrassed by accidentally sending copies of your personal message to a group of people for whom the message was never intended. On the other hand, if you are continuing a group conversation, you'll want to be sure that you are replying to everyone.

✦ Read your message before you send it, and ask yourself if you'll regret it later. Most systems do not allow you to take back (cancel) what you've sent.

The intention here is not to dissuade you from using e-mail; rather, it is to ensure your effective, educated use of it. E-mail is a very powerful and useful Internet tool in the hands of responsible users.

USING THE E-MAIL FEATURE OF NETSCAPE

Starting with Navigator 2.0, Netscape can both send and read e-mail. As was noted earlier, it works in the POP mail client/server environment. That is, the Netscape mail feature is a POP mail client and requires a POP mail server to be running on the host computer where you have your account.

NOTE: Before you can use this feature on Netscape, you need to specify the POP mail server name and your user account through the Options menu. Refer to the appendix for assistance.

ENTERING THE E-MAIL ENVIRONMENT

From the Window menu, select Netscape Mail (Windows) or Mail (Mac).

On a Windows machine, a Password Entry dialog box similar to the one shown in Figure 6.3 is displayed.

If you are using the Mac version or if your password is rejected, select Get New Mail from the File menu or click on the Get Mail button.

The program asks for your password.

FIGURE 6.3

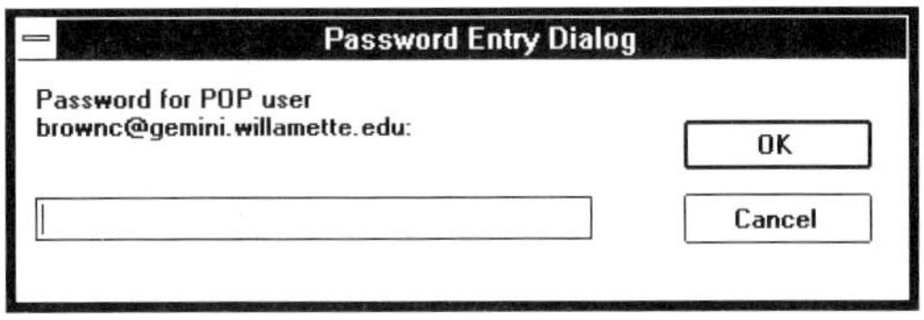

Password Entry Dialog

Password for POP user
brownc@gemini.willamette.edu:

OK

Cancel

Each time you start the e-mail environment, the program asks you to enter the password. This is the password for your account on the host computer.

 Type in the password and click OK.

The e-mail screen is displayed, similar to the one shown in Figure 6.4. Remember, the screen displayed here is for the Windows version. The Macintosh screen uses slightly different icons and column headings.

Notice that the screen is now divided into three sections, called *panes.* The Mail Folder pane on the top left contains various folders, including ones marked Inbox and Trash. The Message List pane on the upper right displays the contents of the selected folder. The Message Text pane at the bottom will display the contents of the selected mail.

The relative size of the panes can be adjusted by dragging the pane dividers. When you have a folder name that is very long, for example, you may not be able to read the entire name. In this case, you will need to make the folder pane a little wider so that you can see the names of the mail folders. If you have only Inbox and Trash folders, this should not be a concern.

First you will send an e-mail message to yourself to make certain that there is an incoming message to read.

FIGURE 6.4

Column header

Mail Folder pane

Message List pane

Pane dividers

Message Text pane

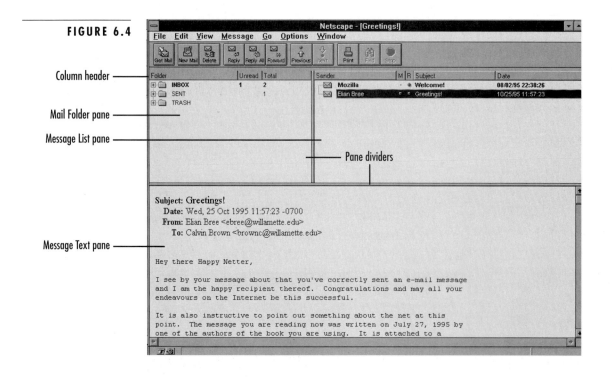

SENDING AN E-MAIL MESSAGE

To send an e-mail message, select New Mail Message from the Message menu or click on the New Mail button. You will see the already familiar Mail Document dialog box. As before, your name already appears in the From field. You can enter the recipient's address in the To field, then enter the appropriate information in the Subject field and the mail text. When ready, just click on the Send button.

 Send an e-mail message to yourself.

CHECKING FOR INCOMING MESSAGES

To view any incoming messages, select the Inbox folder in the Mail Folder pane. All the messages in the Inbox are listed in the Message List pane.

NOTE: If it's been a while since you last received messages, you may want to select the Get Mail command again so that mail is transferred from the POP server to your computer. Beware: your computer will receive all e-mail that was stored in the POP server—even the ones you had already received the last time you gave the Get Mail command.

 Select the Inbox folder by double-clicking on it.

The Message List pane displays the header information of all e-mail messages already in the Inbox, as shown in Figure 6.5.

In the list, green buttons appear next to unread messages. As soon as you read the message, the button disappears. Notice also that the pane contains several columns. The first column lists the subject, the fourth column shows who sent the message, and the fifth column shows the date of the message. If the column width is too narrow, then drag the right edge of the column header to make it wider.

FIGURE 6.5

Sender	M	R	Subject	Date
✉ **Mozilla**	·	✱	**Welcome!**	**08/02/95 22:38:26**
✉ Elian Bree	·	·	Greetings!	10/25/95 11:57:23
✉ Calvin Brown	·	·	Hello from Me	10/25/95 12:06:48

READING AN E-MAIL MESSAGE

To view a message, all you need to do is double-click on it in the Message List pane. If you haven't already, you should receive an e-mail message back from yourself, or from Elian Bree. You may have to use the Get New Mail command again.

 Double-click on a message in the Message List pane.

The Message Text pane displays the e-mail content, as shown in Figure 6.6.

REPLYING TO AN E-MAIL MESSAGE

To reply to a message displayed in the Message Text pane, select Reply from the Message menu or click the Reply button. A new composition window appears with the sender's address automatically in the To field. You can include the original e-mail text by pressing the Quote Doc (Windows) or Quote (Mac) button. Again, you can edit the quoted text to display just the pertinent information.

FORWARDING A MESSAGE

At times you may want to forward the displayed message to others. From the Message menu, select Forward or click the Forward button. A new composition

FIGURE 6.6

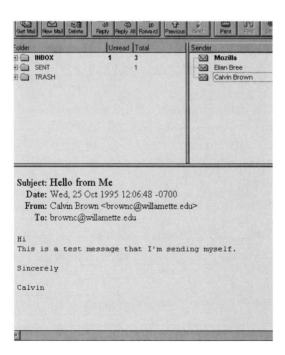

window is opened with the cursor on the To field. The original message is sent as an attachment to the current mail. You can add your own message and send it on.

SAVING MESSAGES

Let's say that you want to place all messages from Elian Bree in a special folder called "Elian."

From the File menu, select New Folder.

A prompt appears asking you to enter a folder name.

Type **Elian**, and click on OK.

A folder called Elian appears in the Mail Folder pane.

Make sure that the Inbox folder is selected, and highlight the message from Elian Bree in the Message List pane.

If you are using the Windows version, from the Message menu, select Move. A pop-up menu appears, listing all folders. Select the folder Elian.

If you are using the Macintosh version, drag the message from Elian Bree into the Elian folder.

The mail message has been moved to the Elian folder.

Let's verify this.

Double-click on the Elian folder.

The message from Elian appears in the Message List pane.

DELETING MESSAGES

As mentioned earlier, messages are stored indefinitely in any mailbox until you explicitly delete or transfer them to another folder. When you delete a message from a folder other than the Trash folder, that message is moved to the Trash folder. Until you explicitly empty the trash, the message is not deleted. So if you inadvertently delete a message that you wish to keep, you can select the Trash folder, find the message there, then move it to another folder.

NOTE: When you delete a message in the Trash folder, it is really deleted.

Select the Elian folder.

Select the message from Elian Bree, then click on the Delete button.

The message is moved to the Trash folder. You can verify this if you want.

To explicitly empty the trash, from the File menu, select Empty Trash Folder.

EXITING THE E-MAIL ENVIRONMENT

 From the File menu, select Close.

You return to the Web browser.

SUMMARY

In this chapter, many of the terms and concepts necessary to use e-mail are introduced:

✦ E-mail is a system for sending messages or files to the accounts of other computer users.

✦ Many Web browsers allow you to send e-mail messages. Some require that you specify a valid e-mail address for yourself.

✦ An e-mail URL has the format of mailto:*user-address*.

✦ Advantages offered by e-mail can also be drawbacks. Hence, one must learn effective use of e-mail.

✦ Release 2 of Netscape lets you read received e-mail in a POP mail environment.

KEY TERMS

address   e-mail (electronic mail)   POP (Post Office Protocol) mail

REVIEW QUESTIONS

1. How can you tell if an URL is for sending an e-mail?

2. What is the standard format for an e-mail address on the Internet?

3. Is there an easy way to find someone's e-mail address?

4. What do you need to know to send an e-mail message?

5. What are the two parts of an e-mail message?

EXERCISES

1. Send an e-mail message to your instructor.

2. Locate an e-mail URL. What Web page was it on? To whom was it addressed?

3. Find the e-mail address of your Congressperson and send a message.

DISCUSSION TOPICS

1. Why would someone put an e-mail URL on a Web page?

2. How would you go about finding an e-mail address for a friend?

3. What are some ways you can convey a "mood" through an e-mail message?

USENET NEWSGROUPS

7

CHAPTER

OBJECTIVES

Upon completing the material presented in this chapter, you should understand the following aspects of the Internet and Usenet newsgroups:

◆ The concept behind Usenet
◆ How to use the newsgroup feature in Netscape
◆ How to find a newsgroup
◆ How to subscribe and unsubscribe to a newsgroup
◆ How to read news articles
◆ How to respond to news articles

WHAT'S USENET?

Suppose for a moment that you have a wide selection of newspapers from which to read right at your fingertips. These papers might range from serious national and international newspapers to local school papers to supermarket tabloids. Imagine browsing these papers, scanning for your favorite topics, reading bits here and there, and maybe even cutting out the articles you find interesting. Now suppose that not only can you *read* these newspapers, you can also *reply* to them. You can even start a new topic of discussion. This is what **Usenet** is all about: It is a collection of thousands of topically organized **newsgroups** in which you can find information and discuss almost any subject.

Thousands of people are already participating in these Usenet discussions, and their number is growing each day. In order to participate, however, one must have a news reader program. Netscape, in its attempt to be a very comprehensive Internet tool, of course incorporated the newsgroup feature!

NOTE: If you are using a Web browser that does not support newsgroups, you may want to use other news reader programs, such as NewsWatcher for Macintosh or WinVN for Windows.

Although newsgroups are often referred to as just plain **news**, they aren't at all the same as a newspaper, where an editor controls what people write. Although your site can, for a fee, pick up a news feed from a commercial service such as Clarinet (which distributes United Press International and other wire services electronically over Usenet), the vast majority of the information on newsgroups is written by users on the Internet discussing topics that interest them.

WHO MANAGES NEWSGROUPS?

Anyone on the Internet can start a newsgroup on any topic of interest. Sometimes there is a **moderator**, someone who reviews the **articles** before they are distributed, but most groups function as an open forum on a topic, much like what you might hear if the participants were gathered together in someone's home, talking over their favorite beverage. The topics of discussion can range from nuclear physics to artificial intelligence to vegetarian recipes for chili or the latest soap opera. In fact, articles in a newsgroup may not even stay on the supposed subject of the group. No one person or organization controls or regulates newsgroups. For the most part, they are an open and uncensored environment. They are a good place for browsing and don't require a lot of commitment.

News is received through **newsfeeds**. At each site, a person or a group known as the **news administrator** is responsible for what newsgroups a site receives and how the newsfeed is operated. A site may choose to restrict the flow of news or to receive every conceivable newsgroup. A typical site may subscribe to up to 2,000 newsgroups.

The news administrator also decides how long to keep news articles. This depends on factors such as the amount of local space available to store the newsgroup articles and the amount of traffic on the particular newsgroup. A news article may be stored for just a few days or for months. If you don't look at a newsgroup for awhile, you will miss topics of discussion as they come and go.

NEWSGROUP ORGANIZATION

There are literally thousands of newsgroups, and new ones appear daily. Also, as mentioned earlier, they do not necessarily contain "news" as we usually think of it. These are essentially discussion groups, though some are devoted to classified ads, announcements, or just plain old bulletin-board services. Fortunately, the topics are broken down by groups, so you can select the ones of most interest to you. Group names are often three or more words long, separated by periods. The first word provides a very general description of the group, and each following word becomes more and more specific. For example, the newsgroup named *sci.bio.ecology* stands for a *sci*ence group, focusing on *bio*logy, with an emphasis for *ecology*. You could reasonably expect to find discussions of the effects of acid rain on lake fish or the decline of songbirds in North America in this newsgroup. Table 7.1 lists some types of newsgroups.

There are many other "top level" designations that you will run into. For instance, some schools have newsgroups for different topics on campus, and these will have their own local hierarchy. Willamette University has a set of newsgroups that start with "willamette," such as willamette.news or willamette.forsale, where the campus community can share information of local interest.

TABLE 7.1 SOME TYPES OF NEWSGROUPS

alt	*alt*ernative, and sometimes silly or extreme discussion.
bit	*bit*net listservs—many listservs are available via Usenet. The names follow a bit-listserv.listname scheme.
clari	*clari*net news service—a newswire service for which you must pay. You may or may not have access from your site.
comp	*comp*uter topics, including use, purchase, and programming.
de	*de*utsch—technical, recreational, and social discussion in German.
gnu	discussions related to the Free Software Foundation (FSF) and its *GNU* project.
K12	for students in *K*indergarten through *12*th grade, or discussions about that group on the 'net.
misc	*misc*ellaneous—meaning exactly that! This contains newsgroups that don't fit under other headings.
news	*news*groups! Yes, these are newsgroups *about* newsgroups! Despite how ridiculous this may sound, groups such as news.newusers.questions might actually be a good place to start.
rec	*rec*reational groups, including pastimes and sports groups.
sci	*sci*ence topics—these can range from the very simple to the very sophisticated.
soc	*soc*iety, including foreign countries and cultures. Many of these lists are in foreign languages.
talk	*talk* about a number of different topics, including philosophy, politics, and religion. Discussions are often influenced by current events.

NOTE: In a newsgroup name, a period is read as "dot." For example, "willamette.news" is read "willamette-dot-news."

USING THE NEWSGROUPS FEATURE

Before you can use Netscape's news reader feature, you will need to have specified the news server (the computer used for the newsfeed) you are using. In addition, if you want to **post** to a newsgroup—that is, start your own discussion or reply to someone else's posting—you must have a valid e-mail address. This is done through Mail and News on the Options menu. See the appendix for directions.

Netscape's newsgroups feature is very easy to use, yet robust. The interface is very similar to the Mail window, and includes many of the same features. Once you subscribe to a newsgroup, Netscape keeps track of the news items you have already seen and displays new items that have arrived since your last session. The program even lists newly formed newsgroups and asks if you are interested in reading them.

STARTING THE NEWSGROUPS FEATURE

 Click on the Newsgroups button, or from the Window menu, select Netscape News in the Windows release; in the Macintosh release, this item is called News.

The Netscape News page, similar to Figure 7.1, is displayed. The Macintosh screen uses slightly different icons and column headings than the ones shown here.

The available news servers are listed in the left window pane. If more than one news server is listed, click on the name of the server that you entered in the Directories section of the Mail and News dialog box on the Options menu.

The Netscape News window is composed of three window panes. The left pane is for the names of newsgroups, and the right pane will display a list of the articles of the newsgroup you select. The lower pane is for the text of an article which you select. The size of each pane can be changed by dragging the pane dividers with your mouse. The individual column widths can be adjusted by dragging the column borders, or placed in a different order by dragging the column labels. The display of the panes is highly dependent on your choice of pane width, column width, and overall size of the Netscape window. You may have to make some adjustments in order for your display to more closely resemble the figures shown here.

 Change the size of each window pane so that your screen approximates the one shown in Figure 7.1.

FIGURE 7.1

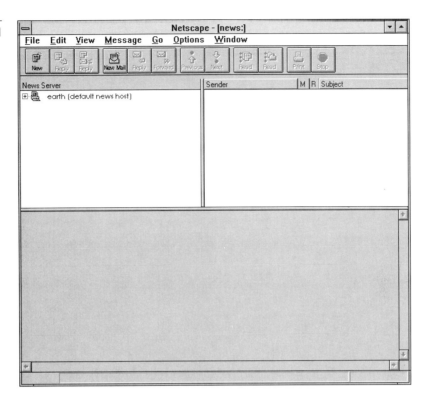

 Try dragging one of the column labels to a different position. If your column labels are not in the same order as those shown in Figure 7.1, move them so that your column labels match those in the figure.

If you or someone else who used this program on your machine already has subscribed to a newsgroup, the name will appear in the left window pane when you first view the Netscape News window.

FINDING NEWSGROUPS OF INTEREST

 From the Options menu, select Show All Newsgroups. If this option is dimmed in the Macintosh release, double-click on the news server icon, which appears at the top of the group column in the left window pane. Also, if this is the first time you have viewed all newsgroups, you will get a message informing you that it may take Netscape a few minutes to save a copy of the Newsgroups list. In Windows, click on OK to proceed; on a Macintosh, click on Yes.

All the newsgroups available at your site are displayed, similar to Figure 7.2.

FIGURE 7.2

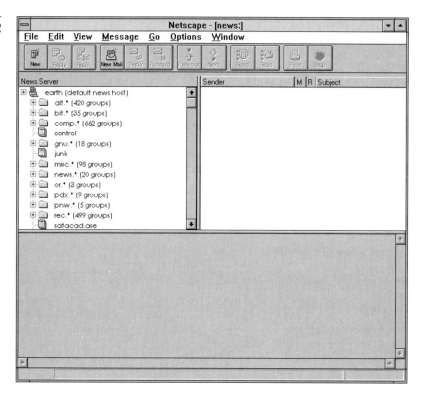

The Newsgroups list is organized by newsgroup type as described earlier. Anytime you see "*" at the end of a name on the Newsgroups list, there will be a further subdivision of newsgroup names, since "*" is a wildcard.

 If necessary, widen the column in the left window pane listing the top-level designations so that you can read them. For example, if you see alt. at the top of the list, widen the column until you see alt.*.

Click on rec.*. You may have to scroll down a bit to find it.

All newsgroups that start with rec. are displayed under the rec. folder.*

You may still see some names that end with an asterisk. That means there will be still further subdivision of those newsgroup names. You can return to the previous display by clicking on the Back button.

To **subscribe** to the newsgroup, click the boxes in the Subscribe column for all of the newsgroups to which you want to subscribe.

Let's say that you are interested in a newsgroup on oceanography. You could take a look at the science category—groups that have *sci* as the first syllable in their names.

Click on the sci.* folder.

Newsgroup names starting with sci. are displayed.

Scroll the screen until you see the sci.geo.* folder, then click on it.

You will see a newsgroup called sci.geo.oceanography in the list of sci.geo. groups.*

OPENING A NEWSGROUP

Once you locate a newsgroup you want to read, you can open it by double-click-ing on the newsgroup name.

Double-click on a newsgroup of your choice.

A screen similar to Figure 7.3 is displayed, listing articles posted to the newsgroup. You may want to resize the right window pane to make the articles list easier to read.

As you can see in Figure 7.3, Netscape also **threads** the articles in each news-group. The lead article in a thread is indicated by a pointer icon in the Windows release and by an open folder icon in the Macintosh release. Threading displays ar-ticles grouped together based on a particular topic and the replies that have been

FIGURE 7.3

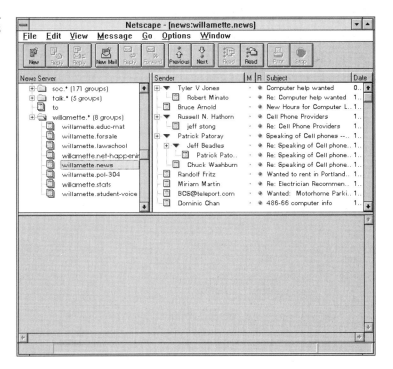

posted on that same topic, with the replies indented under the original article. This format allows you to read news items in order, based on what appears as the subject line of the article. While newsgroups organize articles loosely by subject, threads further organize them by collecting all articles in a subject group that have the same subject line.

Notice the buttons that appear at the top of the Newsgroups window. In Navigator 2.0 (beta), some of these buttons have the same names but different functions, as indicated by the individual button icons. These buttons appear in five groups as follows:

Group 1

These three buttons deal with the newsgroup you are currently reading:

	New	You can post a new article to the newsgroup.
	Reply	You can post a reply to the article you are reading.
	Reply	This button was not implemented in Navigator 2.0 (beta), but is intended for posting to the group and replying via e-mail to the author of the article you are reading.

Group 2

These three buttons are for e-mail:

	New Mail	You can also send regular e-mail from the Newsgroups window.
	Reply	You can reply only to the author of the message you are reading.
	Forward	You can forward the article you are reading to someone else via e-mail.

Group 3

These two buttons are for moving back and forth in the list of articles:

	Previous	You can go to the previous article in the newsgroup you are reading.
	Next	You can go to the next article in the newsgroup you are reading.

Group 4

These two buttons allow you to mark articles and threads:

	Read	You can mark the selected thread as read. You can also mark individual articles as read without opening them by clicking on the green button next to the subject line.

Read	You can mark all articles and threads as read.
Print	You can send the selected article to your printer.
Stop	You can stop loading the article you selected.

READING AN ARTICLE

To read an article, double-click on the name of the article. The article is displayed in the message text window pane in the lower part of the newsgroup screen.

Double-click on the article.

A screen similar to Figure 7.4 is displayed.

Use the scroll bars in this window pane to scroll the screen as you read the article. You can use any of the Newsgroup buttons described above at any time as you are reading the articles.

FIGURE 7.4

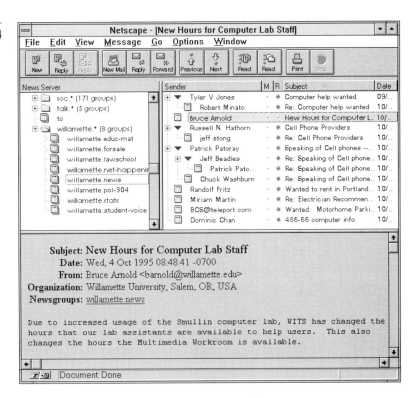

RESPONDING TO AN ARTICLE

If you've just read an article to which you really want to respond, you can send a private message to the author of the article and/or post a response to the newsgroup for everyone to read.

There is one thing you need to remember as you send a reply. The Netscape program automatically inserts the sender's address—your address. The address it uses is the one that you indicated in the Identity section of the Mail and News dialog box on the Options menu. So if you are using your friend's computer to read the news, you should be careful before sending a response to a news article, as your friend's e-mail address will appear as the sender.

Don't post a message to the newsgroup unless you have something to say that would be valuable to all readers. If you are responding to an article, take time to decide whether the reply should go to the original author rather than to the entire list. Also, it is a good idea to include parts of the original article in your response so that it will be easier for readers to understand to what issue you are responding.

 To post your response on the newsgroup, have the article displayed on the screen, then click the Reply button ⬛.

To send a reply via e-mail to the original author, click on the Reply button ⬛.

In all cases, the window is similar to the one shown in Figure 7.5. The header information will vary depending on whether you are posting to a newsgroup or sending an e-mail message.

FIGURE 7.5

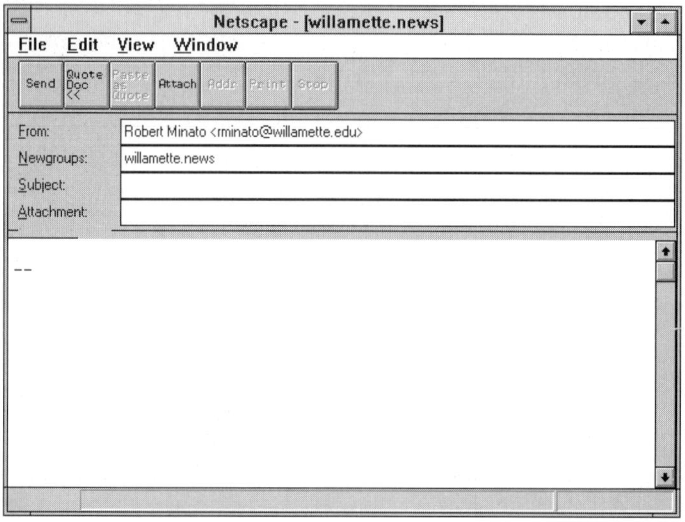

![Netscape - [willamette.news] window with File, Edit, View, Window menus. Toolbar buttons: Send, Quote Doc <<, Paste as Quote, Attach, Addr, Print, Stop. From: Robert Minato <rminato@willamette.edu>; Newsgroups: willamette.news; Subject:; Attachment:]

Notice that some of the header fields are already filled in with information from the article you are responding to. To include the original article in your response, click on the Quote Doc button. You can edit the article to insert your message. When you are ready to send the message, click on the Send button.

NOTE:	If you find an article you'd like to send (forward) to a friend, you can use the Forward button, . You will have to fill in the Send field with your friend's complete e-mail address.

POSTING A NEW ARTICLE

To post a new article, click on the New button, . The Compose Message screen is displayed with the newsgroup name already in the Newsgroups field. You can enter your own subject in the Subject field. You know how to do the rest.

QUITTING NEWSGROUPS

When you are finished reading the news, choose Close from the File menu. Choosing Exit from this menu will end your Netscape session. You can also click the Close box if you are using a Macintosh, or double-click on the Control menu icon if you are using Windows.

WORDS OF ADVICE

One thing you may want to do when you first subscribe to (or start reading) a newsgroup is observe and find out the tone and flavor of the newsgroup. Each newsgroup has a different personality and, often, its own set of etiquette rules and protocol. It's good to find out these things before posting. The name of the newsgroup can be quite misleading. If the newsgroup did not turn out to be what you had in mind, simply **unsubscribe** (or stop reading).

As with any group of people, there are sometimes inappropriate, if not downright nasty, exchanges on newsgroups. These are sometimes referred to as **flame wars**. If you notice these, it is best not to get involved. If you feel you want to say something, send a personal message to the individual. Being involved in a flame war can be a fantastic waste of time, and does no good for your Web reputation! You never know where your message may end up, and imagine your surprise when, years from now, you are on a job interview and your potential employer says, "Hey, aren't you the person who ranted and raved on . . ." As mentioned before, think twice before posting a message. Sometimes folks on a list will surround their extreme comments with "flame on" and "flame off," just to let others know that they are aware of what they are doing.

Also, when new users join the group, they often ask questions that have been asked and answered several times in the past. This can become tiresome for long-time followers of the group. To help out the new readers and to prevent the same topics from being discussed ad nauseam, most newsgroups have a list of **Frequently Asked Questions (FAQs)**. These are usually posted to the group once every three to four weeks so that new users can find them. You may want to hold off posting a question to a group until you have read its FAQs.

Posting to a newsgroup is really no different from sending e-mail. Be very aware that your message can end up in some surprising places. Never send anything that you wouldn't want the world to see. In general the Internet is a friendly place with lots of people ready to help each other with problems, questions, and conversation, and it is up to us to keep it that way.

| **BOX 7.1** | **JUST THE FAQs, JACK** |

A curious phenomenon associated with newsgroups is that as new groups of people join, they invariably ask the same questions that the last group of people to join the newsgroup asked. Instead of answering these questions again and again, the long-term subscribers of a newsgroup often cooperatively put together a list of "Frequently Asked Questions," or FAQs.

Even though FAQs are put together on a volunteer basis, they are almost always a rich source of (usually) valid information. There is no way of guaranteeing the authority of the answers in FAQs, but consider this—if anyone did supply the wrong answer for a frequently asked question, several other people would probably correct it immediately.

If you are looking for basic information on a particular subject, you may want to invest some time in finding the newsgroup FAQ that deals with that subject. Usually the FAQs are posted every few weeks on a newsgroup.

Also, FAQs are archived at the FTP sites, such as rtfm.mit.edu and pit-manager.mit.edu. FTP is discussed in Chapter 4, along with specific examples involving retrieving FAQs. Another source of FAQs is through the WAIS index, usenet.src, which indexes all the FAQs stored at pit-manager.mit.edu.

SUMMARY

In this chapter, many of the terms and concepts that are necessary for you to read Usenet news are introduced:

◆ Usenet is a collection of thousands of topically organized "newsgroups."

◆ Newsgroups are a forum for free expression, with no one controlling or regulating the discussion.

◆ News articles are received through newsfeeds. A news administrator at each site determines which newsgroups are received.

◆ Newsgroups are organized into categories, as described by the first word of their name.

◆ News reader programs help keep track of news items you have already seen and display new news and newsgroups as they appear. They also let you respond to articles by sending e-mail either to the person who posted the article or to the entire newsgroup.

KEY TERMS

articles	news	subscribe (to a newsgroup)
flame war	news administrator	threaded
Frequently Asked	newsfeed	unsubscribe (from a
Questions (FAQs)	newsgroups	newsgroup)
moderator	postings	Usenet

REVIEW QUESTIONS

1. What is a newsgroup?

2. Who controls newsgroups?

3. What does a news administrator do?

4. How are newsgroups organized?

5. What does it mean to subscribe to a newsgroup?

6. How would you go about finding a newsgroup dealing with Japanese culture?

7. Can you read the news articles of a newsgroup to which you have not subscribed? Explain.

8. What options do you have for responding to a newsgroup article?

9. What is a thread? How do you display or read all articles in a thread?

10. What's a FAQ?

EXERCISES

1. Go to the misc.test newsgroup. Read the articles and submit a follow-up posting. Submit a copy of the posting.

2. Find the names of two newsgroups on the topic of education. Describe them.

3. You've heard that there are some newsgroups especially established for questions and answers about the different "hierarchies." Find and read postings to these newsgroups and describe their contents.

4. Find a discussion group about some aspect of your ethnic background or a culture that interests you. What is the name of the newsgroup? Discuss some interesting postings.

5. Find a newsgroup that is primarily in a language other than English. Name the newsgroup and the language used.

DISCUSSION TOPICS

1. Is Usenet a valid resource for information? How would you use it?

2. As a new reader of a newsgroup, why is it a good idea to wait a bit before participating in a discussion?

3. Do you think newsgroups should be more tightly controlled? Should they be censored?

CREATING YOUR OWN WEB PAGE

8

CHAPTER

OBJECTIVES

Upon completing the material presented in this chapter, you should understand the following aspects of the Internet and using HTML:

✦ The concept behind HTML

✦ How to create an HTML document

✦ Design issues related to a Web page

✦ Copyright and other laws affecting the 'net

HYPERTEXT MARK-UP LANGUAGE

After exploring the Web for a while, you might decide you would like to author one of these Web pages yourself. In other words, you may want to publish your information for others to view. The way you can do this is to create documents in **HTML**—the **HyperText Mark-up Language**. HTML is the coding language for Web pages. "Mark-up" is an old publishing term referring to typesetting instructions that were written in the margins, "marking up" the original document. An HTML document is just a regular text document, except that special elements called **tags** are inserted to indicate information about formatting and positioning of links. Let's look at an HTML document.

Access the Web page http://www.willamette.edu/~kpitter/sample.html.

A sample Web page, similar to the one in Figure 8.1, is displayed.

When you display a Web page in Netscape, you can also view what the HTML document, or the **source document** for the Web page, looks like.

 From the View menu, select by Document Source.

The source document for the Web page is displayed, similar to the one in Figure 8.2.

NOTE: Did you notice the other option, by Document Info? This option displays information about the current Web page, such as URLs of all the links used, when the page was last modified, and the security level, as shown in Figure 8.3. At the time of writing this book, there is no way to return to the original Web page from the Document Information display other than to restart Netscape. You can try this on your own.

At first glance, a source document may be quite confusing because of the tags that are inserted to indicate formatting information and link information. These are the words enclosed in < > brackets, such as <title>, <h1>, and <li>. Some tags work in pairs to affect the text enclosed between them, while others work singly.

FIGURE 8.1

FIGURE 8.2

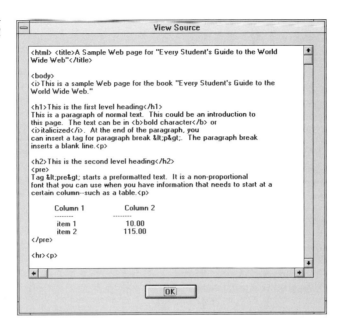

For example, the tags <title> and </title> work together to identify the enclosed text as a title. Similarly, <b> and </b> indicate that the enclosed text is to be bold. On the other hand, a single tag <p> denotes the end of a paragraph (so a line break and a blank line are inserted). Tags can be entered in upper- or lowercase letters. Therefore, <p> and <P> both specify the end of a paragraph.

NOTE:

Viewing and formatting a source document definitely is *not* a case of WYSIWYG (what you see is what you get). Tags dictate how the source document will display as a Web page. For example, pressing the ENTER key twice to insert a blank line between paragraphs in the source document has no effect on the Web page. To insert a paragraph break on a Web page, you need to insert the <p> tag.

HTML is not that difficult to learn. You can be up and running in less than an hour. Although there are a number of HTML editors (software created specifically to develop a Web page), all you need is a simple word processor. You can then insert tags to indicate how you want the page to look and which words should be links. When you are finished, save the document as an ASCII, or text, file. Table 8.1 on page 111 shows the basic HTML tags. The word processor you use does not have to be sophisticated—any text editor will do. In the Windows environment, you can use Notepad, which comes in the Accessories group; in the Macintosh environment, SimpleText will do fine, although neither of these editors will allow very large documents.

FIGURE 8.3

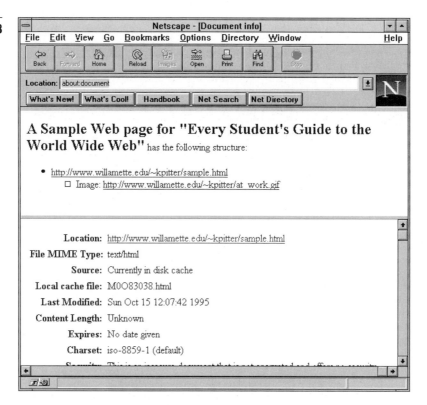

CREATING A WEB DOCUMENT

You will now put together an HTML document which you will save on the computer you are using (PC or a Macintosh) or on a floppy disk. This HTML document will contain links to URLs that were used in previous chapters in this book. You can access this HTML document from Netscape.

Start your favorite word processor, Notepad, or SimpleText.

Type **<title>** to indicate the beginning of the title. Do not press RETURN.

You are to type a title that you want to appear on the Title Bar when you open this Web page. The title you enter should be less than 60 characters in length because of the size of the Title Bar. If you want the entire title to fit in the Bookmarks menu, it should be under 45 characters in length. Since you are creating a Web page that will access Web pages used in this book, let's try "Web Pages for Every Student's Guide to the WWW."

Type **Web Pages for Every Student's Guide to the WWW**. Now type **</title>** to indicate the end of the title.

The document should look similar to the following.

<title>Web Pages for Every Student's Guide to the WWW</title>

Press (ENTER) to move the insertion point to the next line.

Although pressing (ENTER) has no effect on the appearance of the final product, it helps you to visualize the final Web page and clarifies the content of the source document.

Now you want to enter a heading for the Web page. This heading does not have to be the same as what appears on the Title Bar. Since it is the main heading to display on the Web page, you will make it a level 1 heading.

TABLE 8.1   THE BASIC HTML TAGS

TAG	MEANING
<Title>*text*</Title>	*Text* appears as the title at the top of the screen.
<H1>*text*</H1>	*Text* appears as the Level 1 Header (largest). This indicates a section heading in your document. There are six levels of headers in all (<h1> to <h6>).
<P>	Paragraph break—indicates a break between two paragraphs of text. A carriage return and a line feed are inserted.
 	Line break—this forces a line break with no extra space between the lines.
<HR>	Horizontal rule—this inserts a horizontal divider line to create a visual break between sections of your document.
<A HREF="http://some.url.here/">*text*</A>	Hyperlink anchor—this allows you to make a link to other documents and external images—the magic that makes hypertext work! *Text* becomes the underlined word that serves as the link.
<IMG SRC="image.gif">	In-line image—this allows you to include images in your document.
<LI>	Indicates an item on a list.
<OL><LI>*item 1*<LI>*item 2*...</OL>	The <OL> tag means an Ordered List. *Items* on the list appear on separate numbered lines.
<UL><LI>*item 1*<LI>*item 2*...</UL>	The <UL> tag means bulleted list. *Items* on the list appear bulleted on separate lines.
<B>*text*</B>	*Text* appears bold.
<I>*text*</I>	*Text* appears in italics.
<U>*text*</U>	*Text* appears underlined.

Type **<h1>Web Pages to use with "Every Student's Guide to the World Wide Web"</h1>** and press ENTER.

You will now insert some text to explain what this Web page is about:

 Type text to describe your Web page. Make sure to insert a **<p>** at the end of the description. Also, if it runs more than one paragraph, insert a paragraph break, **<P>**, at the end of each paragraph. The following is a sample.

> This Web page has a dual purpose. One is for practice on how to create an HTML document, but it also can be used to access all URLs listed in the book "Every Student's Guide to the World Wide Web" by Keiko Pitter and Robert Minato.<P>

Let's insert a horizontal line here to separate what you just entered from the rest of the document.

 Type **<hr><p>** to insert a horizontal line and a paragraph break (blank line), and press ENTER.

Now you will list Web pages mentioned in each chapter. Let's think about what you will list without regard to HTML tags or URLs for Web pages. The list could be one of actual URLs, but titles will help the viewers more. You may want to list them as follows:

> CHAPTER 1
> *Chapter 1 did not contain any URLs.*
> CHAPTER 2
> Netscape's Welcome page
> Apple Computer
> FBI
> The White House
> CHAPTER 3
> Data Research Associates
> Hytelnet
> Car System Database
> (and so on)

Another way is to introduce the titles in a narrative:

> CHAPTER 1
> Chapter 1 did not contain any URLs.
> CHAPTER 2
> Chapter 2 started with the **Netscape's Welcome** page. In discussing URLs for Web pages, **Apple Computer**, **FBI**, and **The White House**

were used as examples.

CHAPTER 3

This chapter covered the use of Telnet URLs. We Telnetted to the database **at Data Research Associates** to search for books written by Jack Kerouac. Also, **Hytelnet**, which is a search tool for Telnet resources, was introduced. It also covered the use of **Carl System Database**.

(and so on)

In either example, the underlined words are links that will allow readers to connect to those resources.

Next you will enter the heading for Chapter 1. Since you used a level 1 heading for the page, you will need a level 2 heading for each chapter. These chapter headings are subheadings of the page heading.

 Type **<h2>Chapter 1</h2>** and press ENTER to enter the heading for Chapter 1.

Since there is no URL listed in the first chapter, you will indicate this by using italic characters. Remember, characters enclosed in <i> and </i> appear in italics and <p> indicates the end of a paragraph (inserts a line break and a blank line).

 Type **<i>Chapter 1 did not contain any URLs.</i><p>** and press ENTER.

Now enter the heading for the second chapter.

 Type **<h2>Chapter 2</h2>** and press ENTER.

Following the first example, you want to make a bulleted list of sources.

 Type **<ul>** and press ENTER to indicate the beginning of a bulleted list.

Type **<li>The Netscape Welcome Page** and press ENTER.

Similarly, list Apple Computer, FBI, and The White House.

Then type **</ul>** and press ENTER to indicate the end of this list.

Your document should look similar to the following

<title>Web Pages for Every Student's Guide to the WWW</title>
<h1>Web Pages to Use with "Every Student's Guide to the World Wide Web"</h1>
This Web page has dual purposes. One is a practice on how to create an HTML document, but it also can be used to access all

> URLs listed in the book "Every Student's Guide to the World Wide
> Web" by Keiko Pitter and Robert Minato.\<P>
> \<hr>\<p>
> \<h2>Chapter 1\</h2>
> \<i>Chapter 1 did not contain any URLs.\</i>\<p>
>
> \<h2>Chapter 2\</h2>
> \<ul>
> \<li>Apple Computers
> \<li>FBI
> \<li>The White House
> \</ul>

In this same manner, you can enter a list of Web pages for Chapters 3 through 7.

At the bottom of a Web page, it is a good idea to state the name of the person who created the page and the date. Let's insert a horizontal line, then enter this information in italics.

Type **\<p>\<hr>\<p>** to insert a blank line, a horizontal line, then a blank line.

Type **\<i>Created by *yourname*\
today's date\</i>** to insert your name and the date in italics.

When finished, save the document on a disk (either on the hard drive of your computer or on a floppy disk) as a text document. If you are a Windows user, use the extension .htm. If you are a Macintosh user, use the extension .html for the filename. That is, if your filename is "myweb," use myweb.htm if you are a PC user, and myweb.html if you are a Mac user. And remember, you need to save the file as a text file.

NOTE: If you are using NotePad or SimpleText, you can just do a Save. With other word processors, you need to use the Save As command and indicate the file type as "text." If you are not sure how this is done, ask your instructor.

Make sure to close the document (so it is no longer displayed on the screen).

The document you have created is an HTML document. However, it does not contain any links. Let's view it as a Web document.

Start a Netscape session.

From the File menu, select Open File.

You will see an Open File dialog box similar to the one shown in Figure 8.4.

FIGURE 8.4

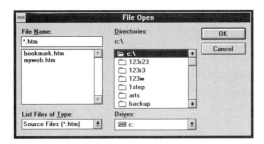

Enter the disk and directory (folders) where your HTML document is stored, then type the name of the file in the File text box.

Your Web page is displayed, similar to Figure 8.5.

You should be proud of yourself for creating a Web document.

CREATING LINKS

Now you want to make some of the text into links.

Start your text editor/word processor again and open your Web document.

FIGURE 8.5

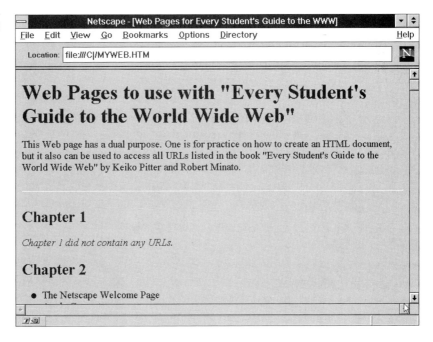

You will now make a link out of "Keiko Pitter." Remember, links appear as underlined words. When "Keiko Pitter" is selected, the viewer can see Keiko Pitter's home page. The format for a link is *<a href="external file">text</a>*, where *external file* is the URL of the file to which you are linking and *text* is the text that is to appear underlined.

 Position the insertion point just before the word "Keiko" in the description section.

Type **<a href = "http://www.willamette.edu/~kpitter/">**.

Position the insertion point just after the word "Pitter."

Type **</a>**.

The sentence should look as follows:

> . . . by <a href="http://www.willamette.edu/~kpitter/">Keiko
> Pitter</a> and Robert Minato.

Save, then close the document.

Start Netscape and open your HTML document file.

Your screen now looks similar to Figure 8.6.

FIGURE 8.6

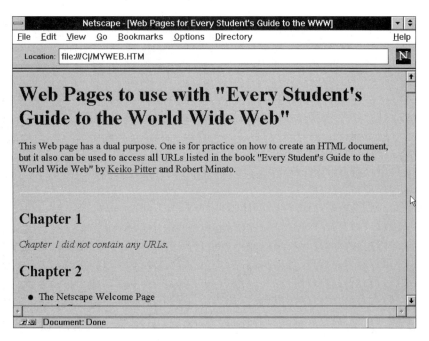

Notice that the text "Keiko Pitter" is now underlined. It is a link.

Select the link <u>Keiko Pitter</u>.

The home page for Keiko Pitter opens.

Now edit your HTML document again. Make "Robert Minato" into a link. The URL for Robert Minato's home page is http://www.willamette.edu/~rminato/.

Similarly, make other Web pages into links. In each case, note their URLs. Then enter **<a href="***URL***">** just before the text you want made into a link, and enter **</a>** just after.

Save and close the document again, making sure that it's saved as a text file.

Go back to Netscape, and if the Web page is already on display, click on the Reload button. If not, open your HTML file.

Displayed Web pages contain several links, indicated by text that is underlined.

Try clicking on various links and make sure that they work. If you notice a problem, check for spelling errors. URLs can be tricky.

ADDING IMAGES

The next thing you probably want to try is to include images on the Web page. There are two ways to do this: as an **in-line image**, meaning it appears on the Web page as the page is loaded, and as an **external image**, meaning you click on a link to a separate page where the image is displayed. In either case, the image must be stored in the **GIF (graphics interchange format)** format. For the best (fastest) result, the GIF file should be located in the same directory (folder) as your HTML document.

IN-LINE IMAGE

The format for the tag for an in-line image is <img src="*filename*.gif">, assuming the file appears in the same directory (folder) as the HTML document. The GIF file can be located elsewhere on the Internet, in which case you need to specify the complete URL for the GIF file. The drawback in not having the image in the same directory (folder) as the HTML document that references it is that it takes longer to load. Furthermore, if the computer on which the image resides is down, you cannot load the image. Right now, since you may or may not have a GIF file on your directory (folder), you will use an image that is kept elsewhere. The image will be a small one.

BOX 8.1

GIF FILES

A graphics file contains data that, when interpreted properly, presents an image. This image may be a photograph, a drawing, or something else entirely. It may have as few as two colors or, theoretically, as many as 16 million (16 million is the limit of human perception. This is referred to as *true-color*).

There are many different types of graphics files. Each type was developed for a specific use or by a manufacturer who was unhappy with what was available at a particular time. Some of the types have built-in limitations, such as the number of colors, that prohibit their use in high-quality production. Others take advantage of new technologies that were not available when the earlier standards were set.

The choice of graphics file to use is often made for you by the application you are using. The Web uses a format called GIF, which stands for Graphics Interchange Format. (Or the JPEG format may be used if you are certain only Netscape users will be viewing the Web page.) The GIF format supports up to 256 unique colors from a palate of 16 million. Originally published by CompuServe, it is a very common format, often seen on the network for pictures and weather maps. It uses a compression scheme to reduce file size.

Given a graphics file of any type, you can convert it to GIF format. Several conversion programs are available for both Mac and PC systems.

Start your text editor or word processor and open your HTML document.

Position the insertion point just after </a> following "Keiko Pitter."

Insert the following: **<img src="http://www.willamette.edu/~kpitter/ commie.GIF">**.

Save and close the file.

Start Netscape, if not already started.

Open your HTML document. If it was left open, then click the Reload button.

The displayed document has an in-line image displayed, similar to Figure 8.7.

EXTERNAL IMAGE

An external image is an image opened as a separate page. Hence, the tag is the usual external reference tag with the format <a href="*filename*.gif">*text*</a>, where *text* is the word that appears as a link. Again, if the GIF file is in the same directory (folder) as the HTML document, the retrieval is faster. Otherwise, it can take a long time, and as before, you will need to specify the complete URL.

FIGURE 8.7

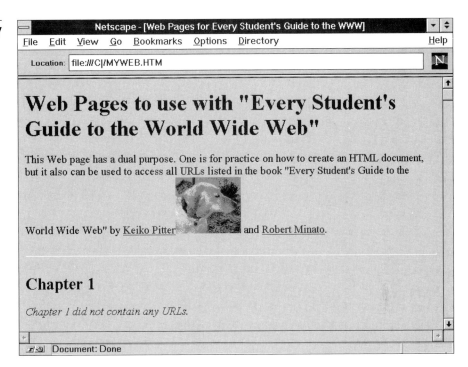

```
Netscape - [Web Pages for Every Student's Guide to the WWW]
File   Edit   View   Go   Bookmarks   Options   Directory                    Help

Location:  file:///C|/MYWEB.HTM
```

Web Pages to use with "Every Student's Guide to the World Wide Web"

This Web page has a dual purpose. One is for practice on how to create an HTML document, but it also can be used to access all URLs listed in the book "Every Student's Guide to the

World Wide Web" by Keiko Pitter and Robert Minato.

Chapter 1

Chapter 1 did not contain any URLs.

```
Document: Done
```

Start your text editor or word processor and open your HTML document.

Again, position the insertion point at the end of the paragraph.

Insert the following: **If you want to see a photo of Robert Minato, click on <a href="http://www.willamette.edu/~kpitter/portia.GIF"> this</a>.**

Save and close the file.

Start Netscape, if not already started.

Open your HTML document. If it was left open, then click the Reload button.

A screen similar to Figure 8.8 is displayed.

You should notice that the word "this" is underlined to indicate a link. When you position the mouse pointer over it, the status bar at the bottom displays the URL for the image file. If you click on "this," a Web page displaying the image opens.

You can click on the link to access the image. However, be forewarned that loading an external image can take a while. If you decide you don't want to wait, click on the Stop button.

The hands-on lesson for this chapter is over. You can continue to explore the Web or close and exit Netscape.

FIGURE 8.8

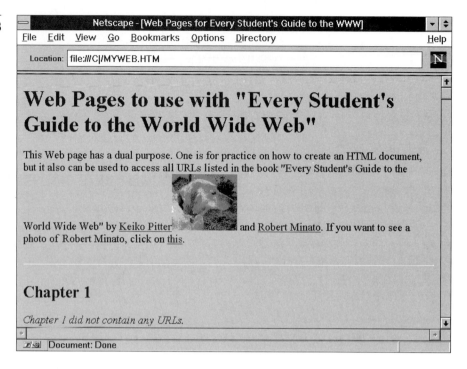

NOTE: To publish your Web page on the Internet so the whole world can view it, you need to place your HTML document on a Web server. You'll need to contact your local computing support staff to find out if a Web server is already available for use or if one can be made available.

NOTE: You might have wondered about audio and video files that can be added to a Web page. The concept is the same as that of a GIF file. In a Mac environment, you can utilize these files on just about any computer. On a PC, however, the use of a sound or video card is required.

DESIGN ISSUES FOR THE HOME PAGE

Technology makes it easier and easier for anybody to create a "professional" looking document—meaning documents that include various fonts, graphics, and colors. However, this empowerment has not been without problems.

In traditional print publishing, experts are used for various components of publishing: a writer, an editor, graphics designer, layout designer, printer, and so on. Each one of these people used his or her expertise and tools of the trade to

contribute to the final product. Current technology makes it possible for one in
dividual to create a document from top to bottom, but that individual may not
have expertise in all the components of publishing. You may have noticed, as you
see countless desktop publications, that the quality of these documents varies
greatly as a result of the newfound power of technology. Likewise, as you surf
through the various Web sites, you will notice that some Web pages are artfully
conceived and beautifully executed, while others come up woefully short in
terms of aesthetics and leave logic behind in terms of organization. Even if you
are creating a Web page to be used by you and you alone, a well-designed home
page will pay off by being easy to use. Here are some things to think about when
designing a Web page:

1. *Go easy on the images.* The price of using an image is high. The larger the
   image you add to your page, the longer it takes a Web browser to load it. The
   greater the number of images, the more that factor becomes multiplied. It is
   true that if you keep image files in the same directory (folder) as your HTML
   document, it doesn't take as much time to load. However, graphics files take
   up a lot of storage. So if you do want to link to larger image files, set them up
   as external images so a viewer has the option of not loading them. By the way,
   the same is true for sound and video files.

2. *Avoid frequent font changes.* HTML allows you great control over the fonts
   you use. You can set up six levels of headers and use italics and boldface. But a
   document that changes fonts in every paragraph or so is distracting. While it
   is effective to use italics and bold for emphasis or clarity, use them in mod-
   eration.

3. *Less is more.* A cluttered home page is not only difficult to read; it also makes
   it almost impossible to find the information you need. Consider breaking
   your links into categories and moving information to separate pages (separate HTML documents).

4. *Remember the dynamic nature of the 'net.* There is nothing more frustrating
   than selecting a link only to get an error. If you are using links in your Web
   page, test them from time to time and make sure that they still work. Because
   you need to update your Web page all the time, make sure the design of the
   page is flexible enough to allow easy changes.

If you'd like to know more about both HTML document construction and layout
design, access the Web page http://www.willamette.edu/html-composition/.
This page contains links to "The Beginner's Guide," "Quick Reference," and
"Composing Good HTML." Another interesting page is the Tips for Web Spin-
ners at http://gagme.wwa.com/~boba/tips.html.

COPYRIGHT AND OTHER LAWS IN CYBERSPACE

Publishing in cyberspace is no different than print publishing in that you need to pay attention to the contents of your publication, including the copyright. For example, if you publish a statement that damages the reputation of a product or a person, you are liable for damages. If you use other people's documents, texts from books, and so on, without first obtaining permission from them *and* giving proper credit to them, you are violating the copyright and intellectual property rights laws.

What makes this so difficult is that electronic technology makes it so easy to copy and paste text or images created by others. It is also very easy to scan graphics images to create image files that can be inserted in the electronic documents. You must remember, however, that the ease with which such tasks can be done does not make them necessarily legal. When possible, get permission. If not, use another image or use another text for which you can get permission.

There are many people who argue that the current copyright and other laws are no longer applicable to the current digital technology, and it is almost certain that these regulations will change. In the meantime, however, you will have to be aware of these regulations and abide by them.

Also, remember that a Web page, once published on the Internet, can be viewed by people all over the world. The recent trend seems to be that local ordinances are used to determine the legality or appropriateness of displayed material. What does that mean? Even if the content of a Web page is perfectly acceptable where you live, viewers from another culture may find it offensive or, in a worst-case scenario, your page could violate local ordinances. This could can get you into hot water! Until local and federal agencies understand the global nature of the Internet and make appropriate provisions, this type of problem is often a possibility. The intent here is not to scare you away from publishing in cyberspace, but to make you aware of some legal implications.

If you are interested in finding out more about these issues, you can access The Copyright Website at http://www.benedict.com/.

SUMMARY

In this chapter, many of the terms and concepts necessary to create your own Web document are introduced:

✦ HyperText Mark-up Language (HTML) is the coding language for Web pages.
✦ HTML uses text-embedded codes called tags to specify formatting and link information. Otherwise, the Web document is just a plain text file.

◆ A tag for a link has the format <a href="*external file*">*text*</a>, where *external file* is the URL of the link destination.

◆ A tag for an in-line image has the format <img src="*filename*.gif>.

◆ In publishing a Web page, one has to be cognizant of various copyright and other intellectual property regulations as well as the appropriateness of published material for other cultures that might view it.

KEY TERMS

external image
GIF (graphic interchange format)

Hypertext Mark-up Language (HTML)
in-line image

source document
tags

REVIEW QUESTIONS

1. What is the relationship between a Web page and an HTML document? Explain.

2. How does HTML specify text formatting?

3. As you look at someone's Web page, can you look at the HTML document behind the page? Explain.

4. What kind of word-processing tool do you need to create an HTML document? Explain.

5. What tags would you insert in a document to link the text "Willamette University" to the Web server www.willamette.edu?

6. What is the difference between an in-line image and an external image?

7. What tags would you insert in a document to link the text "Portia, the cat" to the image file with the URL http://www.willamette.edu/~kpitter/portia.gif?

EXERCISES

1. Create a Web page for an organization to which you belong.

2. Look at source codes for various Web pages. Find and describe features that were not discussed in this chapter.

DISCUSSION TOPICS

1. How does a user go about getting a permission to use an image or text?

2. Study the current copyright regulations. Are they appropriate for the current digital technology? How should they change?

APPENDIX

WHERE TO GET NETSCAPE

You can obtain the latest version of Netscape directly from Netscape Communications Corporation at ftp.netscape.com. Make the connection with your FTP client software, then follow the directions below, depending on your operating system.

Windows

1. Locate the /netscape/windows directory.

2. The latest version will be listed as ns16????.exe, where ???? indicates the version number. For example, version 2.0b is named N16E20B1.EXE.

3. "Get" the file, placing it in a temporary directory, *not* one called C:\NETSCAPE.

Macintosh

1. Locate the /netscape/mac directory.

2. The latest version will be listed as netscape-X.X.hqx, where X.X is the version number. For example, Navigator 2.0b is named netscape-2.0b1.hqx.

3. "Get" the file, placing it on the desktop or in another folder.

NETSCAPE SYSTEM REQUIREMENTS

Windows

✦ 80386 CPU or later

✦ Windows 3.1 or later

✦ 4 megabytes RAM (8 megabytes recommended)

✦ 8 megabytes free disk space (some returned after installation)

✦ Additional disk space for communications software, helper applications, and disk cache

Macintosh

✦ System 7.1 or later

✦ 4 megabytes RAM (8 megabytes recommended)

✦ 8 megabytes free disk space (some returned after installation)

✦ Additional disk space for communications software, helper applications, and disk cache

NETSCAPE CONNECTION REQUIREMENTS

DIRECT CONNECTION VIA LOCAL AREA NETWORK CONNECTED TO THE INTERNET

A direct connection is often available at universities, government offices, and even at some businesses by means of a local area network. This will almost certainly involve some assistance from your system administrator.

Windows and Macintosh

✦ Install a network card in your computer.

✦ Install the appropriate network software on your hard drive.

✦ Obtain a user account and password for the host computer.

INTERNET CONNECTION VIA HIGH-SPEED MODEM

Online service providers that offer SLIP and PPP connections typically provide their accounts with all of the necessary software and instructions for installation. There may be a charge for this software; also, users will generally experience higher monthly fees due to increased connection time once they start using the World Wide Web.

✦ A 14,400 baud modem, or faster, is recommended.

✦ Obtain a SLIP or PPP account with your online service provider.

Windows

✦ Install the Winsock software on your hard drive; Winsock receives the SLIP or PPP communication from your online service provider.

✦ A popular Winsock is Trumpet Winsock, available through many online service providers, or via anonymous FTP at ftp.trumpet.com.au.

Macintosh

✦ Install Mac/TCP on your hard drive; Mac/TCP receives the SLIP or PPP communication from your online service provider.

✦ System 7.5 includes Mac/TCP; it is also available for previous systems from an Apple dealer.

INSTALLING NETSCAPE

The Netscape software is very easy to install on either the Windows or the Macintosh platform. Once you have obtained Netscape over the Internet with your FTP client, just follow these directions, depending on your operating system.

Windows

1. Execute the NS16????.EXE file, in either Windows or from a DOS prompt; this will uncompress all of the Netscape files that are needed for installation.

2. Return to Windows, if necessary, then run SETUP.EXE; you'll see this file in the temporary directory mentioned above. You will be prompted for a directory in which to install Netscape. The default selection is C:\NETSCAPE, but you can install the program in any directory, except the one where the NS16????.EXE file resides.

3. Now just follow a few prompts on the screen, and that's it!

Macintosh

1. Uncompress the file using your uncompression utility program.

2. Double-click the Netscape Installer icon that appears when the file has been uncompressed.

3. Now just follow a few prompts on screen, and that's it!

SETTING UP NETSCAPE

Netscape will start up and run immediately after installation, but you will soon run into problems if you don't get to know your Preferences dialog box. Although this dialog box differs a bit in appearance between platforms, and even between releases on the same platform, all of the essential screens are similar on both Macintosh and Windows. Release 2 for Windows, in beta release at the time of this writing, has adopted the "clickable tab" idea familiar to users of other recent Windows products. Previous versions relied on the "pop-out list" idea first seen in Macintosh software, and later in Windows programs. A common complaint is that items on the various screens are sometimes grouped in ways that make no sense. This has apparently been remedied to a large extent in Release 2, but we'll have to wait for the official release to be sure! Release 2 for Windows is used for the screens shown here, with mention of the differences Macintosh users will see. For additional information on all aspects of installing and using Netscape, refer to the online Netscape Handbook (choose Handbook from the Help menu). Note that

◆ You can make all the changes necessary using the first four items listed on the Options menu.

◆ When you've finished making all of your changes, click on the Save Options item at the bottom of the Options menu.

GENERAL

Appearance tab (Figure A.1)

◆ Make a choice about how you want the Netscape toolbar to appear; the Pictures and Text choice takes up the most screen real estate, while Text uses the least.

◆ Enter a Home Page Location if you like. By default, this is Netscape's home page. You must have the complete URL of the page you want to specify. Not many users choose to start Netscape with a blank page, but that's the other option.

FIGURE A.1

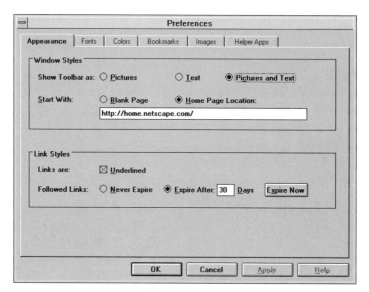

Fonts tab (Figure A.2)

✦ You can select a fixed and proportional font. The fixed font is used where a Web page specifies "preformatted" text. The proportional font is used pretty much everyplace else.

Colors tab (Figure A.3)

✦ Colors are largely a matter of personal taste, although certain combinations would obviously be a problem, such as choosing the same color for Links, Followed Links, and Text, or choosing the same color for Background as for Text color.

✦ It's typical to let Netscape adopt the colors of the page you're visiting, but you can select Always Use My Colors, Overriding Document if you prefer.

✦ The Macintosh release uses pop-out lists for font and color selections, while the Windows version uses buttons to access the lists of choices.

Bookmarks tab (Figure A.4)

✦ Specify the location for your Bookmarks file.

FIGURE A.2

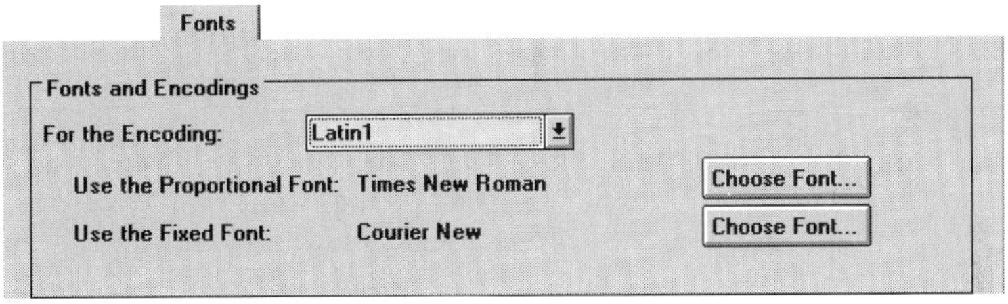

FIGURE A.3

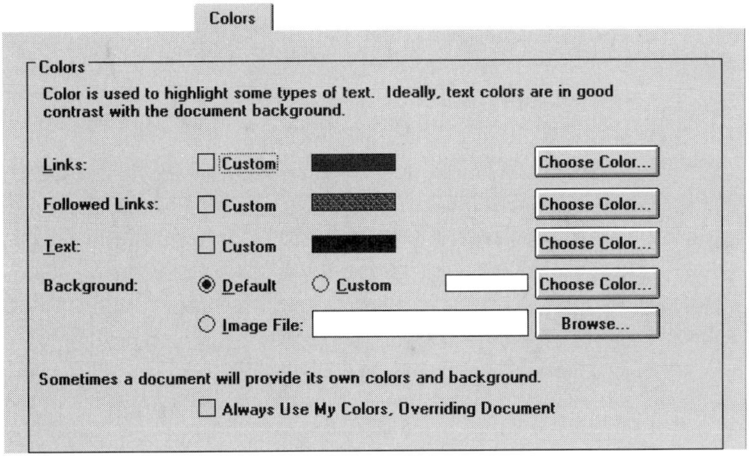

FIGURE A.4

Bookmarks
┌ Bookmarks ────────────────────────────────
The Bookmarks are stored in the file:
[C:\NETSCAPE\20B\bookmark.htm]   [Browse...]

Images tab (Figure A.5)

✦ Allows some control over the method Netscape uses to display images. Most users find the default selections to be appropriate.

Helper Apps tab (Figure A.6)

✦ This dialog box refers to other programs that Netscape uses to display graphics files, run video clips, play sound files, expand compressed files, and other such things from the world of multimedia. Some of these settings depend on

FIGURE A.5

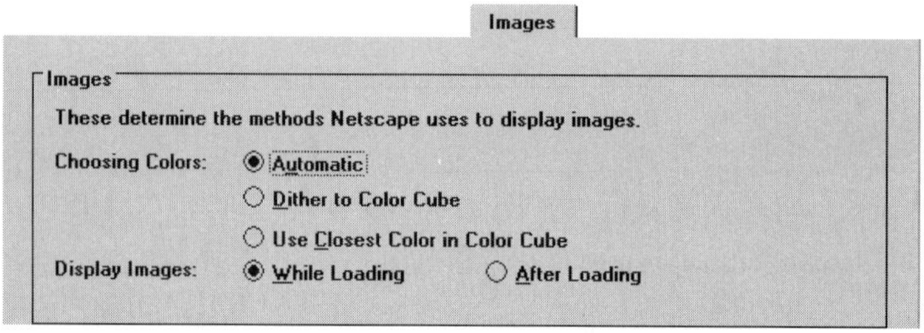

Images

┌ Images ──────────────────────────────────
These determine the methods Netscape uses to display images.

Choosing Colors: ⦿ Automatic
                 ○ Dither to Color Cube
                 ○ Use Closest Color in Color Cube
Display Images: ⦿ While Loading   ○ After Loading

FIGURE A.6

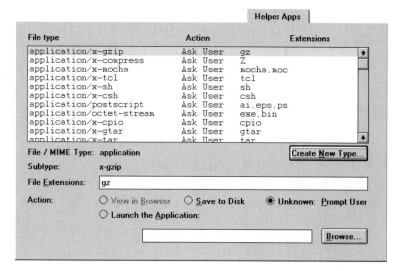

whether or not you've installed devices in your computer capable of dealing with multimedia file types. You should be able to view most Web pages without making any changes, but you may have to install special devices and software to play sound and video files. Refer to the Netscape Handbook and your computer's manual for further information.

Applications tab (Not implemented in Windows Release 2)

✦ You must specify a Telnet application in order to launch a Telnet session from Netscape. If you would like to view HTML source documents with your favorite word processor, you must also specify an application for viewing. In Windows Release 2, these items can be set manually in the NETSCAPE.INI file or in the registry.

MAIL AND NEWS

Appearance tab (Figure A.7)

✦ Specify default settings for fonts and text styles on Mail and News screens.

Composition tab (Figure A.8)

✦ The Send and Post radio button is generally set to Allow 8-bit. Mime compliant has to do with sending formatted files across the Internet. Refer to the Netscape Handbook or ask your system administrator or online service provider for detailed information.

✦ Specify a default address and/or file location for copies of outgoing messages.

FIGURE A.7

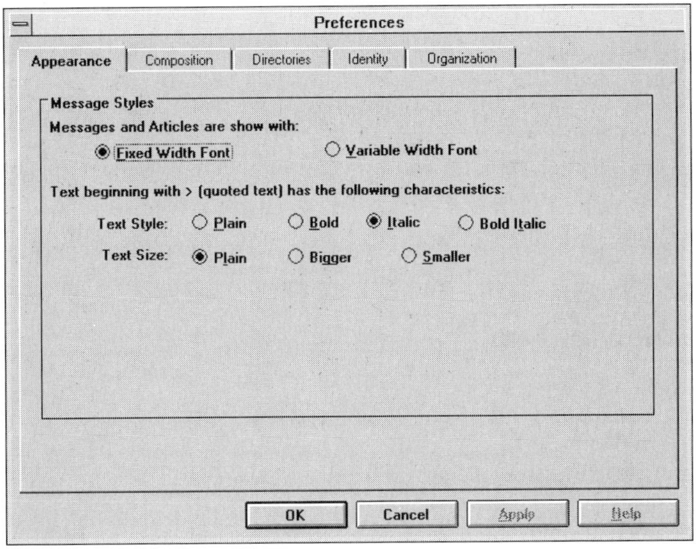

Directories tab (Figure A.9)

✦ Specify your mail server; you will need to obtain this information from your system administrator or your online service provider.

✦ Specify your news server; you will need to obtain this information from your system administrator or your online service provider.

✦ You can also specify a location for your mail directory if your system allows use of Netscape for reading your e-mail. Windows users can also specify their news directory. In the Macintosh release, the news preferences are automatically stored in the System folder.

Identity tab (Figure A.10)

✦ Enter your name, your complete e-mail address, and your organization, if appropriate. In the Macintosh release only, enter your POP user ID. For example, the POP user ID for the e-mail address kpitter@willamette.edu is kpitter.

✦ Specify the location of your e-mail signature file. The Macintosh version has a radio button with a Browse button for locating the file; the Windows version has a box and the Browse button.

Organization tab (Figure A.11; not available in Macintosh version 2.0b)

✦ Specify threading and sorting preferences for your mail and news articles.

Cache and Connections tabs (Figures A.12 and A.13)

✦ The default settings for all of these items will probably work, but you can make adjustments if necessary. Refer to the Netscape Handbook for detailed

FIGURE A.10

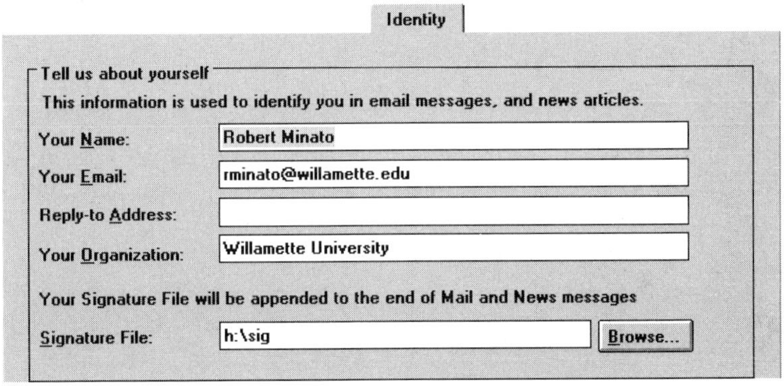

| Identity |

Tell us about yourself

This information is used to identify you in email messages, and news articles.

Your **N**ame: Robert Minato

Your **E**mail: rminato@willamette.edu

Reply-to **A**ddress:

Your **O**rganization: Willamette University

Your Signature File will be appended to the end of Mail and News messages

Signature File: h:\sig   Browse...

FIGURE A.11

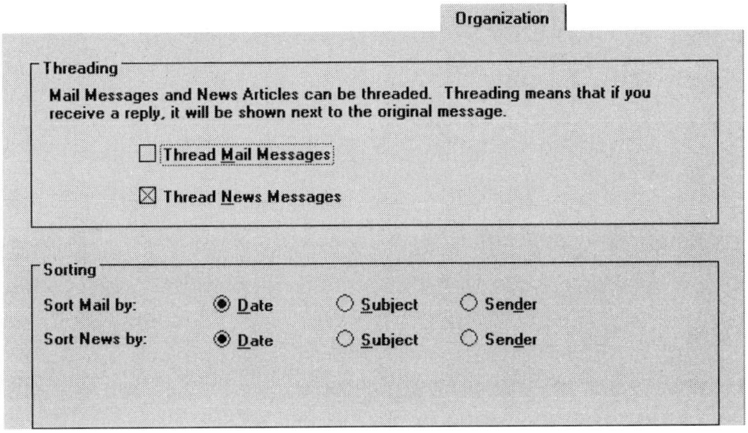

| Organization |

Threading

Mail Messages and News Articles can be threaded. Threading means that if you receive a reply, it will be shown next to the original message.

☐ Thread **M**ail Messages

☒ Thread **N**ews Messages

Sorting

Sort Mail by: ⦿ **D**ate   ○ **S**ubject   ○ **S**ender

Sort News by: ⦿ **D**ate   ○ **S**ubject   ○ **S**ender

FIGURE A.12

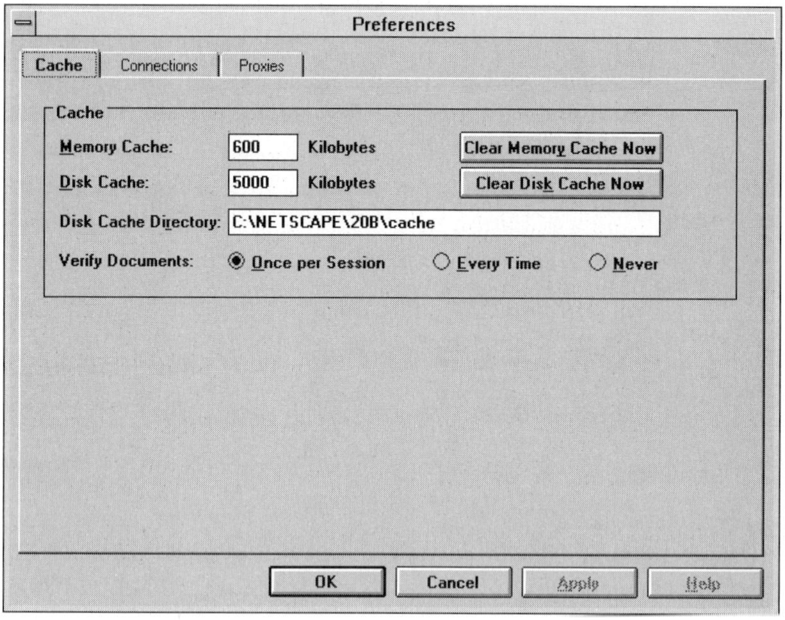

FIGURE A.13

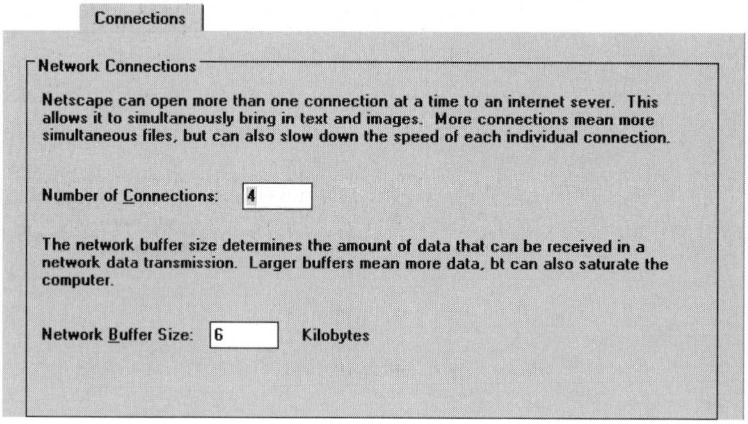

information. You may also have to consult with your system administrator or online service provider.

Proxies tab (Figure A.14)

◆ Setting proxies is required if your Internet connection has a "firewall," which is a networking construct that is intended to keep unauthorized users out of the system. If you are behind a firewall, so to speak, you won't see any Web pages until your proxies are in order. See your system administrator or contact your online service provider for assistance.

FIGURE A.14

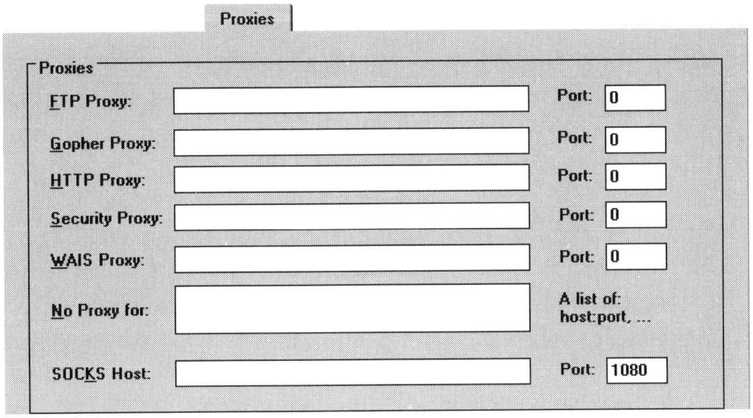

SECURITY

Alerts tab (Figure A.15)

◆ These check boxes allow you to control the display of the Netscape security alert messages that appear when you encounter secure web servers and documents. Click in the check box to enable or disable a security alert.

FIGURE A.15

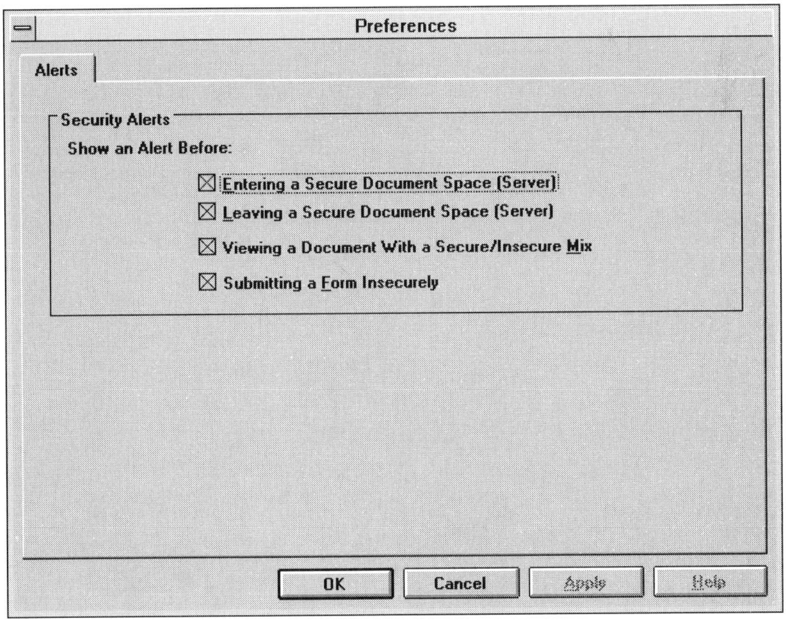

THE HARSH REALITY

Unless you have significant experience with such things, you will likely need some help getting your computer ready for Netscape and the World Wide Web. Readers with direct Internet connections at a university, government, or business location generally have a support person for installing hardware and software and may need only a bit of help with Netscape's Preferences settings. However, users dialing in on a SLIP or PPP connection will face a number of technical hurdles. In addition to getting assistance from your system administrator or online access provider, you may choose to consult one of the many fine books that have been published on the subject of setting up an Internet connection. Some of these books even come with a communications software package on disk. Visit a technical bookstore and you will find at least a shelf or two of them!

GLOSSARY

address Each machine on the Internet has a unique address (*see* "Internet Protocol address"). Furthermore, each user on a machine also has a unique address, usually comprised of a username and domain name, separated by an at (@) sign. For example, a person with the username of portofon on the machine at Willamette University with the domain name of willamette.edu will have the address of portofon@willamette.edu.

anonymous FTP FTP (File Transfer Protocol) is a computer program that allows users to transfer files between machines on the Internet. Anonymous FTP allows user access to remote machines with the login name of "anonymous" for the purpose of transferring publicly accessible files.

Archie Supposedly short for "Archive," this is a program that maintains a database of files on the Internet that are accessible via anonymous FTP.

articles Individual messages in Usenet News. Also referred to as *postings* or *articles*.

ASCII (American Standard Code for Information Interchange) file A standard for representing text in a machine. Many machines can understand ASCII coded files whereas they might not understand files that were coded by programs such as word processors or spreadsheets. However, most programs have an option to save files in ASCII format. ASCII files are sometimes referred to as *text files* or *plain text files*.

BITNET The "Because It's Time NETwork"— an e-mail and file-sharing network used by a large number of academic and research institutions. There are many mail gateways between the Internet and BITNET.

bookmarks A feature found in Gopher and Netscape that lets you keep track of a site or Web page you found useful or interesting.

Boolean A method of searching for information, often used in databases and online library catalogs, using the Boolean operators AND, OR, and NOT.

browser The client for WWW.

browsing A method of finding material in any of the various Internet services by making a selection and seeing what options are displayed. Although it may not appear to be very sophisticated, it is often surprisingly effective, especially in cases where there are few other search methods available.

Campus Wide Information System (CWIS) A software system for electronically providing information of interest to the members of a particular community, most frequently a college or university. Increasing number of CWISs are developed using Gopher.

client A computer or process that relies on the resources of another computer or process (server). The client for WWW is called a browser.

client/server model   The software configuration in which there are two parts to the program: the server, which holds the data; and clients, which can query and retrieve the data from the server. It does not matter if the client and server reside on the same or distant machines.

compressed files   Files that have been compacted to allow for faster transfer or distribution. These files need to be uncompressed before they can be used.

CSO server   A searchable index, usually found on a Gopher, that provides information about users at the particular site.

domain name   The Internet convention of constructing a name for a computer on the Internet. Domain names were created for human use (substituting for numeric IP addresses, which people often find tedious).

external images   Images on a Web page that reside as a link. The link must be selected before the image can be viewed. Compare with "in-line images."

FAQ   *See* "Frequently Asked Questions" list.

File Transfer Protocol (FTP)   A protocol that allows a machine on the Internet to receive or send files to another machine.

flame war   A Usenet phenomenon in which two or more persons get involved in postings that are intentionally inflammatory, derogatory, or argumentative—not a particularly enjoyable or productive activity.

Frequently Asked Questions (FAQs) list   Pronounced FACKs list, it contains often asked questions and answers about a particular subject or area of knowledge. A FAQs list is usually posted to a Usenet newsgroup to save people from asking the same questions over and over again.

FTP   *See* "File Transfer Protocol."

Full Group list   A list of all available newsgroups.

full-privilege FTP   Using File Transfer Protocol (FTP) to send or receive files on a machine for which you have an account, rather than using FTP anonymously. The user has direct access to his or her files. *See also* "anonymous FTP" and "File Transfer Protocol."

GIF (Graphics Interchange Format)   A graphics format used by the Web. That is, an image must be saved in GIF format before it can be inserted on a Web page.

Gopher   A document delivery system for retrieving information from the Internet. The information is stored on Gopher servers and retrieved by Gopher clients. The name Gopher comes from the mascot of the University of Minnesota, which developed the system.

GopherSpace   Everything and anything that is available from all the Gopher servers on the Internet—which is a lot of information. Usage examples: "I found it in GopherSpace!" or "Search GopherSpace for it."

hierarchical file structure   A method of storing files in directories and subdirectories in a hierarchical fashion. The hierarchical structure can be conceptualized as a tree, with a trunk (directory), branches from the trunk (subdirectories), and branches from branches. The leaves at the end of the branches are the files themselves. The user is allowed to organize the files in any logical hierarchical structure desired.

home page   The first document a Web browser will start from. The home page usually contains references to documents of common interest. Browsers allow the user to get to the home page of any WWW document.

hostname   The portion of the domain name that refers to the host itself. For example, in the domain name of jupiter.willamette.edu, jupiter is the host name within the willamette.edu domain.

HTML   *See* "Hypertext Mark-up Language."

hypertext   More than plain text—a document that contains links to other documents and allows the user to move easily from one related document to another. A hypertext book might have sections linked with excerpts from another book.

HyperText Mark-up Language (HTML)   The hypertext document format used by the World Wide Web.

Hytelnet   Peter Scott's database of public Internet sites. Hytelnet includes libraries; Campus Wide Information Systems (CWISs); Gopher, WAIS, and WWW systems; Freenets; and more.

in-line images   Images on a Web page that appear as a part of the page, not separate from it. Compare with "external images."

Internet   A collection of networks using TCP/IP protocols to communicate. The uncapitalized form, "an internet," refers to any collection of networks that can intercommunicate.

Internet Protocol (IP) address   A numeric address in the format *www.xxx.yyy.zzz* that is assigned to a machine on a TCP/IP network. Each IP address is unique and refers to a specific machine on the Internet. An example address would be 158.104.1.1. The periods are read "dot." *See also* "domain name."

IP   *See* "Internet Protocol."

keyword   A word that is relevant to the information sought.

links   The information that a client program (such as Gopher or Netscape) uses to get resources from server programs. A link has all the information necessary for the client program to contact the correct server and request the desired information.

logout   The process of getting disconnected from a computer system.

lurk   Observe without participating.

matrix   Word referring to all the networks in the world, including the Internet and other commercial networks.

moderator   One of several names for a program that sends e-mail to and from a particular list of subscribers.

netiquette   Network etiquette—a proper way to behave on the 'net.

netnews   *See* "news."

news   Officially known as *Usenet,* also as *newsgroups,* a collection of thousands of topically organized electronic forums.

news administrator   The person at an Internet site who is responsible for the care and feeding of the news programs and the newsfeed.

newsfeed   The source (generally another Internet host) for news articles and groups.

newsgroups   The individual electronic forums that are part of Usenet. An individual newsgroup will often at least attempt to have a fairly narrow and defined subject area demonstrated by its name: for example, rec.arts.brewery or sci.botany.

page   A Web screen.

phone book   A queriable database of persons at a particular site, listing whatever information (e-mail addresses, phone numbers, positions) is deemed important.

plain text file   *See* "ASCII file."

platform   A particular variety of computer. Macintosh, Windows, and UNIX are examples of different platforms, each having its own features that differentiate it.

port   The communication channel on a computer that one Internet program uses to communicate with another. A Gopher client hails a Gopher server on a specific port, commonly port number 70.

post, postings   An article or message to a newsgroup, reminiscent of posting a bill or leaflet to a bulletin board or other such public physical information forum.

protocol   A set of rules that allows different machines or pieces of software to coordinate and communicate with each other without ambiguity.

root Gopher   The first menu that appears when you start a Gopher client program. This is the point from which you start accessing all other Gopher selections.

router   A device on the network that moves data from one network to another.

server   The distribution side of the client/server model. A server is a program that holds information, providing it to clients on request.

source document   The HTML document for a Web page.

subject tree   A Gopher server with a menu organized by general subject heading, much like a library.

subscribe   To sign up to receive information from the Internet. You can subscribe to newsgroups and electronic mailing lists.

tags   Text-embedded code used in HTML to define formats and links.

TCP/IP (Transfer Control Protocol/Internet Protocol)   A common protocol used over the Internet to provide reliable, ordered, end-to-end transmission of information. The IP allows information to be transferred across the Internet, and the TCP ensures that the information arrives in the correct order.

Telnet   The standard program for logging onto computers on the Internet.

terminal emulation   A process by which a computer acts like a specific kind of terminal when connected to another computer. This is necessary because, before the advent of personal computers, many people accessed a computer through terminals. These terminals typically had special character sequences to move the cursor, highlight text, or provide other functionality for sophisticated text placement. Programs would use the character sequences when outputting. Later, when personal computers became standard, programs were written to act like (emulate) these older terminals so that the personal computers could be used in place of them for accessing other computers. Many emulators mimic the VT100 terminals. The Telnet program is an example of a terminal emulator, and is still used to connect to UNIX machines.

The 'net   One of many ways to refer to the Internet. Others are "Information Superhighway," "Infobahn," and "The Matrix."

threaded   Describes Usenet news articles that have been collected according to their common topic. A "thread" of conversation ties together articles and their responses.

top-level domain   The most general (rightmost) part of the domain name, usually a two-letter country code for the country controlling the domain if outside the U.S., or GOV, EDU, COM, or MIL for government, educational, commercial, or military sites, respectively, within the U.S.

Uniform Resource Locator (URL)   A machine-readable and (some claim) human-readable standard for locating resources on the Internet. An URL describes the scheme for retrieving the information, the Internet host on which the information is located, and the location of the information on that host.

UNIX   An operating system developed in the 1970s at Bell Labs, now one of the most popular for multiple-user computers. It is also one of the most prevalent operating systems on the Internet. The name puns "Multics," an operating system developed at the same time by Bell Labs.

unsubscribe   To indicate that you no longer want to receive information. On the Internet, you can unsubscribe to newsgroups and electronic mailing lists.

URL   *See* "Uniform Resource Locator."

Usenet   The collection of thousands of topically named newsgroups, the computers that exchange some or all of these newsgroups, and the community of people who read or submit items to them. Not all Internet hosts subscribe to Usenet newsgroups, and Usenet newsgroups may be received by non-Internet hosts.

username   A unique identifier for a user—the name by which one has authorized access to a computer system, and the part of an Internet address by which a person or service is known in an Internet address.

Veronica   A searchable index of items available via Gopher. The name is an acronym for "Very Easy Rodent Oriented Net-wide Index to Computerized Archives."

Web   Short for "World Wide Web."

Wide Area Information Server (WAIS)   A method for creating full text indexes of information, then serving that information over the Internet. This is the most popular way of indexing information on the Internet. WAIS-specific clients are available, but WAIS indexes can also be accessed via Gopher and the World Wide Web.

World Wide Web (WWW)   A method for providing distributed information on the Internet. In the World Wide Web, documents are hypertext, which means that they can provide links to other documents. With the advent of multimedia browsing tools such as Netscape, many people feel the future of the Internet lies here.

INDEX

address, 137
  finding for e-mail, 82–83
  See also Internet Protocol (IP) address
anonymous FTP, 48, 137
Archie, 53–57, 137. *See also* File Transfer Protocol (FTP)
ARPANET, 2
articles, 94, 137
ASCII (American Standard Code for Information Interchange) file, 137

BITNET, 137
bookmarks, 23–24, 137
Boolean operators, 26, 137
browser, 5, 137
browsing, 35–36, 137

Campus Wide Information System (CWIS), 34, 138
CARL System Database Gateway, 70–74. *See also* Telnet
CERN project, 3
chat, 6
client, 137
client software, 4–5
client/server model, 4–5, 137
compressed file, 57, 138

copyright and laws in cyberspace, 122
CSO server, 138
CWIS. *See* Campus Wide Information System
cyberspace, 1

design of home page, 120–121
directory, 20
  Gopher, 40, 42
disconnecting, 63
domain name, 18–19, 138
download, 48

e-mail, 2, 77
  composing and sending, 81–82
  cross-platform, 82
  finding addresses, 82–83
  making faces, 84
  message anatomy, 80
  Netscape versions and, 79
  Netscape, using, 79, 85–90
  pointers, 83–85
  URL, 79
electronic mail. *See* e-mail
error messages, 63
etiquette (e-mail), 83. *See also* netiquette
external image, 117, 118–120, 138

FAQs. *See* Frequently Asked Questions
File Transfer Protocol (FTP), 47, 138
　　anonymous, 48
　　compressed files, 57
　　full-privilege, 48
　　host, 56
　　menu icons, 51
　　menu structure, 49–52
　　obtaining software via, 48
　　pub menu, 50
　　URL, 48
flame wars, 103–104, 138
Frequently Asked Questions (FAQs), 104, 138
FTP. *See* File Transfer Protocol
Full Group List, 138
full-privilege FTP, 48, 138
general audience information server, 34

GIF (Graphics Interchange Format), 117, 118, 138
　　URL, 117
Gopher, 31–42, 138
　　directories, 40, 42
　　menu structure, 34
　　page, 32
　　root Gopher, 140
　　search tools, 38–42
　　servers, 32, 34
　　sites, 42
　　URL, 32
　　URLs for Gophers with good subject trees, 35
GopherSpace, 32, 138
　　browsing, 35–36
Graphics Interchange Format. *See* GIF

hierarchical file structure, 138
home page, 7, 120–121, 138
host (FTP), 56
hostname, 139

HTML (Hypertext Mark-up Language), 7, 107, 139
　　adding images, 117–120
　　copyright and legal considerations, 122
　　creating a Web document, 110–122
　　creating links, 115–117
　　home page design, 120–121
　　tags, 107, 111
hypertext, 3–4, 139. *See also* HTML
Hytelnet, 68–74, 139

in-line image, 117–118, 139
Internet Protocol (IP) address, 18, 139
Internet Relay Chat (IRC), 6
Internet, 2, 139
　　chat, 6
　　connecting to, 2
　　error messages, 63
　　uses, 2
　　vs. online services, 3
　　warning, 8–11
IP address. *See* Internet Protocol (IP) address

keyword-oriented indexes, 24–26
keywords, 24, 139
　　Veronica and, 40

laws in cyberspace, 122
links, 7, 115–117, 139. *See also* HTML
login, 67
logout, 139
lurk, 8, 139. *See also* netiquette

MacTCP, 2
making faces, 84
matrix, 2, 139
memex, 3
moderator, 94, 139
Mosaic, 4, 5

'net, the, 2, 140. *See also* Internet
netiquette, 8–10, 139. *See also* etiquette
Netscape, 4, 5–6
   Chat for Windows, 6
   connection requirements, 126–127
   e-mail, 79, 85–90
   home page URL, 6
   installing, 127
   limitations, 7–8
   menu icons, 34
   News, 96–104
   obtaining, 125
   port, 103
   security, 135
   setting up, 127–136
   system requirements, 125–126
   Telnet sessions, 62
   vs. Mosaic, 5
news, 94, 139. *See also* newsgroups
news administrator, 94, 139
newsfeed, 94, 139
newsgroups, 94–104, 139
   advice, 103-104
   buttons defined, 100–101
   post to, 96
   subscribe to, 98
   threads, 99
   types of, 95
   unsubscribe, 103
NSFNET, 2

page, 7, 139
   anatomy, 15–17
   Gopher, 32
   See also home page
panes, 86
   Netscape News, 96
password, 67
phone book, 139

platform, 5, 140
   sending e-mail across platforms, 82
POP mail server. *See* Post Office Protocol (POP)
   mail server
port, 32, 96, 103, 140
protocol, 2, 140
pub menu (FTP), 50
publishing. *See* HTML

root Gopher, 140
router, 140

search tools, 38–42
searching
   Boolean, 26
   keyword-oriented, 24–26
   subject-oriented, 21–23
server, 20, 140
   Gopher, 32, 34
Simplified Veronica, 40. *See also* Veronica
sites (Gophers), 35, 42
source document, 140
subject trees, 35, 36–37, 140
subject-oriented catalogs of information, 21–23
subscribe, 140
   to a newsgroup, 98

tags, 107, 111, 140
TCP/IP (Transfer Control Protocol/Internet
   Protocol), 2, 140
Telnet, 61–74, 140
   CARL System Database Gateway, 70–74
   disconnecting, 64
   Netscape, 62
   problems, 64
   URL, 63
   warning, 62
terminal emulation, 67–68, 140
threaded, 140

threads, 99

top-level domain, 18–19, 140

Transfer Control Protocol/Internet Protocol
(TCP/IP). *See* TCP/IP

true-color, 118

Uniform Resource Locator (URL), 7, 20, 141. *See
also* specific applications

UNIX, 141

unsubscribe, 141
  to a newsgroup, 103

Usenet, 94, 141

user interface, 5

username, 67

Veronica, 38–4, 141
  Boolean searching, 42
  Gopher directories, 42
  keywords, 40
  Simplified Veronica, 40

virtual communities, 8

Warnings
  Internet, 8–11
  Telnet, 62

Web. *See* World Wide Web

Wide Area Information Server (WAIS), 141

window panes. *See* panes

Winsock, 2

World Wide Web (WWW), 3, 141
  browser, 5
  client software, 5
  limitations, 7–8
  origins, 3
  page anatomy, 15–17
  terminology, 7
  URL, 20
  using HTML, 110–122

Yahoo Directory, 21